Kevin Belton's NEW ORLEANS KITCHEN

KEVIN BELTON WITH
RHONDA K. FINDLEY

PHOTOGRAPHS BY EUGENIA UHL

GIBBS SMITH
TO ENRICH AND INSPIRE HUMANKIND

First Edition
22 21 20 19 18   5 4 3 2 1

Text © 2018 Kevin Belton with Rhonda K. Findley
Photographs © 2018 Eugenia Uhl

Published by
Gibbs Smith
P.O. Box 667
Layton, Utah 84041

1.800.835.4993 orders
www.gibbs-smith.com

Designed by Katie Jennings Campbell
Printed and bound in China
Gibbs Smith books are printed on either recycled, 100% post-consumer waste, FSC-certified papers or on paper produced from sustainable PEFC-certified forest/controlled wood source. Learn more at www.pefc.org.

Library of Congress Control Number: 2017952202

ISBN 13: 978-1-4236-4894-9

TO MY MOTHER SARAH, AUNT DOROTHY, AND GRANDMOTHER NAN, WHO TAUGHT ME SO MUCH AT THE KITCHEN TABLE, AND TO THOSE WHO HAVE SHARED THEIR TABLE WITH ME.

CONTENTS

INTRODUCTION
Everything I needed to know about life I learned at my mother's kitchen table.

THE BELTON FAMILY TABLE WAS BLESSED BEYOND COMPARE. And that kitchen table, my mother's desk so to speak, was the table where we gathered to nourish not only our bodies but our souls as well. Eating my momma's amazing food was the background for all the lessons my mother, father, and grandmother Nan taught me. They believed that caring for others through acts of love, respect, and kindness are the three things that are important to a strong family. All of these lessons were learned over gumbo, paneed meat, fried fish, and boiled crabs. That's how I came to understand what soul food really is because my mother cooked with soul, whether it was classy New Orleans recipes or Nan's recipes from her mother, Grandma Sarah in nearby Canton, Mississippi. And of course, I know where those dishes are best eaten—at the kitchen table with people you love.

Sitting at Mom's kitchen table, life got real. My mother had a gift for gab and she exercised that while she chopped, grated, and stirred the pot, so to speak. She would get my Nan going and Dad would kick back and smile as mother and daughter did what mothers and daughters do best. They'd laugh about the day's events, they'd make plans, and most importantly, they would talk about food. Mom would say something to get my grandma started and then it would be nonstop until we finished eating. After dinner I was dismissed to the tub. Mom and my Nan would do the dishes and end the night sitting on the front porch.

My mother and I have similar personalities, and that's where I get my philosophy of life. Her idea about family and gathering around the table, not negotiable by the way, was based on what she saw as her everyday role at home. Her family was going to laugh together and enjoy all of our blessings. Home wasn't just the physical building, the furniture, or the groceries. Home was more about what the people living there did to show each other how much they were loved. Cooking was how she loved.

Of course Mom was there for all of my important events. She showed me how to be my best self. Sitting down at the kitchen table for a meal all together allowed her to share all of herself with us. Anyone was welcome at our table for a serving of my mom's love.

And because she started all of our meals with either a roux or the trinity, I am affected most by dishes that use these culinary techniques. My mother loved me through food. And that love was powerful. That same love was lavished on me and my cousins Lorna and Chet by my Grandma Emily, Aunt Dorothy, and Great-Grandma Sarah. This is why food and cooking means the world to me. It connects me, grounds me, gives me my place in the world, and nourishes my soul.

Every day is a chance to share a meal and your life with your family and friends. It's as simple as being grateful every day and sharing your bounty. I strive to be grateful in real time because things may not be the same tomorrow as they are today. Make those memories every chance you get. That's what my mom taught me. And, my mom taught me well.

Mom's kitchen table is where I learned work ethic. I learned that hard work pays. I also learned that children always come first. My mother and father both had careers, and they worked full-time and more. But I was their priority, and whatever they needed to do to balance, they did. And it seemed effortless. That's why I have such a strong drive to do right by my kids. And by right, I mean I would have dinner on the table and eat with the boys every night. It fed my soul in a most significant way. The gatherings kept us tight and bonded us more deeply than any other activity we could have taken on.

Back in my youth, kids didn't get involved in adult conversations. But that didn't mean you couldn't listen, watch, and learn. I saw and heard everything that was going on. And I can't believe how much I remember and revisit when I make decisions or try to solve issues even today. That goes for cooking, as well. My mom and Nan didn't walk me through step-by-step how to peel crawfish or snap peas. I followed their lead. They made everything easy. Things my parents discussed during dinner or during Saturday breakfast just stuck. It just amazes me how much of life we lived at that table.

You learned economics in the kitchen because that's where Mom and Dad would sit and pay bills on time and in full. That kitchen table was the doctor's office, accounting office, business office, the bank, the therapist couch, it was the tailor shop, and it was the principal's office too, especially when Aunt Dorothy, who was a principal, would come over.

My mother's kitchen table is where we gathered after she suddenly passed away just shortly after I began college at Louisiana State University. It was the most silence I ever felt at her table. And the silence was not something she would have approved of. She would have preferred that we were eating gumbo and making plans. That pretty much sums up her commitment to our soul, nourishing us no matter the circumstances.

I think about that incredible Belton household created by three of the most warm, loving humans that I'm lucky to call my family. They made sure that what happened around that table meant something real for all of us. I

Sarah Thomas Belton and Dorothy Thomas Gougis

think about Mom and Nan daily. They are my kitchen guardian angels. I always wait to the very last second to cut the bananas for banana pudding to make sure they don't turn brown because that was Mom's way. I always have a bowl of cold water ready when I cut potatoes for French fries because Mom and Nan knew this trick was one of the steps to frying the best fries on earth. Recipes that called for parsley meant waiting to add the parsley at the end because Mom knew that's how you get the nice fresh taste. So I always wait until the end as well. All of this was learned around my

mother's 1950s classic chrome kitchen table with the yellow cushions. Three chairs for them and one for me.

Because of its French and Spanish heritage, New Orleans is a predominantly Catholic city. The Trinity, a religious representation of the Father, Son, and Holy Spirit, has deep religious meaning. So it's no wonder that onion, celery, and bell pepper, the three primary ingredients of Creole cooking, is nicknamed the trinity. You know the rule of threes. Without the trinity, you don't have New Orleans cooking. Without it, you miss the soul of the recipe.

The Beltons were a strong trinity. Dad, Mom, and Nan were tight as could be. I was the lagniappe, that little something extra that makes everything complete. As a single father, Kevin, Jonathan, and I were our own trinity. And I followed my family's lesson to gather at the table with my trinity. Thanks to our lagniappe, the boys' maternal grandmother who lived with us and helped me raise them, we were successful at keeping our table blessed.

Today it's still the rule of threes. Monica and Noah join me as part of my latest trinity. And I'm discovering New Orleans all over again as we create our new family memories through food and enjoying New Orleans as they settle in, fast becoming locals. I get the privilege of sharing the table with these amazing and wonderful people who are joining my sons Kevin and Jonathan, my daughter-in-law Christina, and my grandsons Carter and

Cameron as the loves of my life. They are my soul and my family.

The kitchen table was center stage for my life with Kevin and Jonathan. We had some tough conversations at that table, and we shared our successes by enjoying their favorite dishes—Jonathan's Alligator Sauce Piquant and Kevin's favorite gumbo. Today, Monica and I share this same philosophy, so it's very easy to live this mantra with Noah in tow.

I grew up in three kitchens. Three kitchen tables. Three different ways. There's that trinity again.

Grandma Emily, my dad's mom, lived in the heart of the 7th Ward. They had a full house over there with my Aunt Marion and Uncle Norman both living alongside Grandma and Grandpa Oscar, Sr. You'd walk through Grandma Emily's kitchen door and the smells would just hug you. It was that trinity smell of the onion, celery, and bell pepper cooking that propelled you straight to the kitchen. If you smelled a roux, you'd know she had a gumbo on. Grandma Emily's kitchen was the second to the last room in the shotgun house. And the smells grabbed you from the moment you crossed the threshold. It transported me to a comfortable and safe place. The aroma was a soulful hug.

The one thing she cooked that I cannot repeat wasn't a gumbo or redfish court bouillon. Grandma Emily made the most perfect soft egg. Her soft-boiled egg was better than candy. She'd boil it in the shell for how long I don't know. But she'd crack the top off and sprinkle

on a little bit of paprika. She served it to me in a little ceramic egg cup with a spoon. That soft egg for me was better than a hot fudge sundae, a sno-ball, or a banana split. That's sayin' a lot. And to this day, I've yet to duplicate it.

I was lucky to have a seat at her kitchen table with my dad while he enjoyed his favorite dishes cooked by his own mother. And my dad loved her gumbo. She made a hellacious gumbo.

Grandma Emily was still going strong in her eighties and was there for the birth of both Kevin and Jonathan. She fed them both their first gumbo, and what an amazing experience it was to see them eat her gumbo at her kitchen table, the same table in the same house where I had my first 7th Ward gumbo all those years ago.

My Aunt Dorothy and Uncle Chet, along with my cousins Lorna and Chet, lived in Carrollton on Olive Street by Earhart Boulevard. Today that area is known as Hollygrove. And back when Dorothy and Chet got married and moved from Valance Street, everybody joked they were moving from uptown to the country. They were only about 10 minutes away by car.

Aunt Dorothy's kitchen was like a trip to the Ritz. We went over to visit at least a couple times a week. Her kitchen was completely opposite of my mother's kitchen. And I adored it. Aunt Dorothy was exciting and she had flair. Her food and her kitchen shared that same flair. We had a white porcelain sink. Aunt Dorothy's sink was stainless steel. Our refrigerator was normal—freezer on top, fridge on bottom. Aunt Dorothy's fridge had the freezer drawer on the bottom and was like "wow" to me. The single door on top was my exotic destination once I said the obligatory hello to the grownups. Her fridge was the only fridge in my life other than my mother's that I felt free to open without permission.

We would arrive at Aunt Dorothy's and I'd make a beeline to see what little goodies Aunt Dorothy had made that week. I'd read the menu, so to speak, as I perused the interior of the fridge. Then I'd wait with Chet in his room until we were called for a little snack. If I wasn't offered one of the many goodies I was curious about, I'd slyly ask, "Aunt Dorothy what are those little things there in the back?" And of course she'd say, "Those are oyster patties. Would you care for some?" Ah, music to my ears. I'd sit with Chet, Lorna, Mom, Nan, and Aunt Dorothy and marvel at her delicious creations at her kitchen table. Our table at home sat four. Aunt Dorothy's sat six.

My Aunt Dorothy was a well-respected principal in the Orleans Parish School District. She worked very hard to achieve her career goals when it wasn't easy. My memories are of an elegant lady who was beautifully dressed and super pulled together. She wore a mink coat and drove a Cadillac that she worked hard for.

She was the personification of the types of dishes she made; creative and elegant. There was the classic turtle soup made from a Cowan turtle Uncle Chet would bring her as a bonus from his many trips to Lake Pontchartrain, and the other secret fishing spots that yielded a wild haul of redfish and speckled trout. Or the doberge cake that was pulled from the refrigerator and displayed on the counter top under an elegant glass dome, sliced thin and served to us with a little café au lait. To this day, if my cousin Lorna knows you are coming over, you can bet she will have oyster patties and doberge waiting for you just like my Aunt Dorothy.

With a hectic schedule meeting with professional educators from all over the city and her staff as well as attending meeting after meeting of parents and other obligatory career gatherings, Aunt Dorothy perfected the art of making small plate offerings before it was chic. Little desserts, petite oyster patties, and finger sandwiches made with her fresh homemade chicken salad; I was always envious of my cousins Lorna and Chet because they got to eat all of the leftovers from her entertaining.

And then there was her secret stash of Aunt Dorothy's mix that meant she could whip out anything from stuffed bell peppers to a dirty rice in a matter of minutes. Her mix was her secret weapon. She is my hero of a super organized maestro of the kitchen. Aunt Dorothy and her style in the kitchen was the elegance of execution that made a trip to her house more like a trip to a fancy restaurant. The way she presented food inspires me even today, from teaching and education initiatives to plating up dishes for television. I am proud to have learned her special savvy right at her kitchen table.

And then there were summers in Canton, Mississippi, with my Great-Grandmother Sarah in charge of the other side of my family's cooking heritage. Her food was as soulful as it gets. My country roots are deeply ingrained from my experiences seeing her in action in her Canton kitchen—a kitchen and ways so completely different from our seafood-centric, Creole approach to ageless New Orleans dishes.

Sometimes we took the train from New Orleans and sometimes we drove the 212 miles, just me and Nan off to stay with her mother. Grandma

Sarah's kitchen lives in my culinary soul so deeply. It was in Canton where the earth was our grocer. Fresh butter was churned on the kitchen porch. The ice tea was always slow brewed. Juice was always freshly squeezed. Fresh eggs were a 30 second walk to the back of the property to the pristine hen house. The pace slowed way down. And the food was nothing short of mundane for the Canton family tree, but for me it was miraculous.

The house, simple and smart, backed up to a prolific home garden, and the neighbors next door and down the road were my relatives. Sometimes you couldn't even see where one garden stopped and the other began. Like most of us lucky to have relatives who lived in more rural areas, the experiences we share are similar. Fresh and pure living. Tomatoes straight from the vine when sliced tasted like candy. Eggplant bigger than our arms, sliced, salted, and turned into myriad delicious dishes—Eggplant Parmesan, stuffed eggplant, and fried eggplant with the best flavors so you never noticed, or cared, you were eating the same main ingredient for days on end.

It was in Canton alongside my cousins, aunts, and uncles where I learned to dig in the dirt. I knew where food came from. It was never a surprise to me that there might be a little dirt on the potatoes. A bug in the greens? Who cares? Rinse it off. After all, it came from the garden, and we appreciated the symbiotic relationship of all the creatures that worked in Grandma Sarah's garden.

I liken my Great-Grandma Sarah's kitchen to walking through the dirt. No, she didn't have a dirt floor. But what she did have was a deep connection to the earth and an expertise on coaxing a grand garden harvest and turning those fruits and vegetable into something special. Her food had soul. When we sat at her kitchen table you could smell the aroma of the greens and chicken baking. And, you could smell the earth. The aromas permeated everything and it smelled like home.

As I've grown more connected to people and places outside of New Orleans and sat at many kitchen tables throughout my career, I often refer back to a wise person who recently pointed out the trinity of New Orleans culture: food, music, and architecture. You can find this trinity in almost every New Orleans household. A pot simmering on the stove, a little jazz from a radio tuned to WWOZ, and all happening inside a jewel of a home reflecting the architecture and personality of the many distinct neighborhoods in and around New Orleans. It's been like this in one form or another for 300 years.

For me, soul food isn't defined through a nationality or race. Creole food is my soul food. For someone else, a steak off the barbecue speaks to their soul. I believe that soul food is simply this: dishes prepared that define a family or community. It's not a zip code or an area. If your soul food is gumbo and you are making it in Paris, is it still soul food? I say yes. Absolutely! It's that essence of place and life experiences hovering over the table that gives a meal soul. A meal prepared with soul has more to do with the person who shares themselves through thoughtful, meaningfully prepared food with those who take a seat at their table than it does with a kind of food or a location.

I often make an analogy that resonates with me. The kitchen table is the heartbeat at home. And the soul is what happens around that table. You know without the heart working nothing functions right in your body. For most of us in New Orleans, growing up here we knew kitchens were the heartbeat, pumping the lifeblood of the household and the community through our everyday actions.

To really, truly cook with soul you have to love others, respect the ingredients, pull out the big pots, be fearless, and respect culture as you create your dishes. My family made it look simple. And for that I'm grateful. When I need courage, I think back to how blessed our table was and I make sure to reach back to those days around the table and use that wisdom imparted on me with heart and soul.

"Keep the Table Blessed" is my mantra. And I'm blessed to have signed thousands of books with this message. I am who I am as a chef, community leader, partner, and parent through lessons and experiences taught

during my upbringing and through my Creole culture. I challenge you to invite soul in your life through food and the dishes in this book. With respect to my New Orleans culture and to those inspired by New Orleans and Louisiana food, pay homage to your family by remembering your culture, too. The first time I signed a book with my mantra, it was then and remains always, an homage to my mother, grandmother, and dad.

But as time has passed, it has deepened in meaning. It's a thank you to folks who took me under their culinary wing and allowed me to get my footing and soar in the kitchen. Chef Leah Chase, of the famed Dooky Chase, is one of those I owe big thanks to for her blessing to me over the years. The same can be said of Chef Austin Leslie of Chez Helene. And Chef Mike Roussel of Brennan's. Chef Warren LeRuth of LeRuth's and, last but not least, Chef Paul Prudhomme of K-Paul's. What they taught me was more than just about food. They gave me part of their soul.

Inside the pages of this book, I bare my soul. I poured my soul into these recipes and stories. These recipes are the story of my life in New Orleans. It's my celebration of all of New Orleans and the soul of the past 300 years of food, culture, and architecture. I pay respect to the soul ingrained in New Orleans by the Creoles, the Spanish, the French, the Irish, the Germans, the Vietnamese, the Croatians, and the many peoples who landed in this coastal paradise in and around New Orleans. New

Orleans food isn't a singular cuisine; it is the soul of culture from around the world coming together to celebrate the soul of this city. The soul of New Orleans cuisine represents the people, the culture, and those families who come together today to celebrate her cuisine as one of greatest food cities in the United States and the world.

New Orleans brings it all to the table. I'm pleased to have a seat there. Won't you join me?

Lagniappe

Every local is tuned into the lagniappe of life in New Orleans. That little something extra, and for free, that permeates New Orleans culture, be it food, music, shopping, or living. Back in 1883 when Mark Twain wrote about the word lagniappe in *Life on the Mississippi,* Twain embraced the four-day evolution and usage that left him with a new, pronounced addition to his own vocabulary. In Twain's words it was, "a word worth traveling to New Orleans to get." His introduction went something like this: Day 1: Read it in the newspaper. Day 2: Heard it tossed around numerous times in the French Quarter. Day 3: Asked what it meant. Day 4: Became adept in using it. Lagniappe as a word has a hazy origin, but it is universally embraced as a Spanish word from "La Nape" translated loosely means a gift. The French Creoles pronounced the word "lanny yap" and thus today's spelling, meaning, and ingrained usage.

Much like to Twain, and visitors to the Crescent City ever since, New Orleanian's version of free and something extra is a cultural phenomenon in New Orleans that delights even the most jaded local. Think of it like a baker's dozen—thirteen cookies for the price of twelve. As I sit here putting the finishing touches on this book, drinking coffee in Bywater, I'm treated to a lagniappe of free jazz music with an impromptu concert. In the food world, a lagniappe comes in the form of a little tasty tidbit to start a meal, called the *amuse bouche* or happy mouth. That lagniappe of food is that something extra for free. And, so on.

In each chapter I've include a little lagniappe to go with the stories and recipes that highlights a factual bit relevant to ingredients and their significance in New Orleans cooking and culture. For me, lagniappe is specific and unique to my New Orleans. Savor and enjoy.

MY HOMETOWN AND ME

I belong in New Orleans, and not just because I was born here. It's more complicated than that. New Orleans is really part of my DNA and so much so that if asked to describe myself I would say it like this: "My heart is shaped like a fleur-de-lis and it beats to the rhythm of "Tipitina," written by piano virtuoso and New Orleans native, Professor Longhair. If you cut me open, I bleed gumbo. My favorite color is Mardi Gras green. And my last meal would be a fried oyster po' boy."

Over the years, I've had the opportunity to move and even switch careers. Every time I've thought hard about a change of city, I knew that my heart, soul, and life was shaped and formed by the food, music, culture, and strong family ties to my beloved hometown. I'm my best self by simply living here. New Orleans is where I got my shoes planted firmly on the ground to coin a local saying. As I see it, life here in Louisiana is lived full on, especially in New Orleans. It's a 24-hour city. New Orleanians are just loud and proud about our life and lifestyle. And that's because the culture is everywhere, every day.

What you see when you roam the streets of New Orleans are lovingly preserved buildings carrying on the culture, neighborhoods with distinct personalities, special restaurants, and music venues, and oyster houses still shucking oysters the same way it was done 100 years ago. We New Orleanians are still living in New Orleans. The people are the cultural heartbeat and I am proud to call it my hometown.

And being in my hometown means eating. The food is all about traditional ingredients and generational wisdom from our grandmas. We learn to do things "the right way" in the kitchen, which usually means grandma's way. My cousins and I were always included in the kitchen happenings. We heard the family stories, and enjoyed time at the kitchen table where we didn't even realize we were learning to become expert crab pickers. The recipes in this chapter are some of my favorites because they bring the hometown flavor.

LAGNIAPPE

The top culinary banana dish, Bananas Foster, was created right here in New Orleans in 1951. Not just tops, Bananas Foster is the king of New Orleans' desserts and a testimony to the culinary originality of a young Ella Brennan, fondly known as the "grand dame" of New Orleans cooking. In a flourish to create a new dessert for a visiting dignitary, Ms. Ella commandeered the kitchen at Brennan's on Royal Street and combined bananas, sugar, rum, and fire with a bit of finesse, and voilà, a culinary star recipe was born.

MY KIDS' FAVORITES

Some of my most important customers, food critics, and sources of culinary inspiration are my boys—Kevin, Jonathan, and Noah. The recipes in this chapter are their favorites.

Mardi Gras go-cups with cereal and milk for the car ride to school began my early days of fatherhood. If you know anything about Mardi Gras, you know that catching these cups at all the parades sets your household up for the year. Cereal to go. Drinks to go. Gumbo to go. Everything goes in a go-cup. Go-cups are very much a part of New Orleans' culture.

With that being said, I have to admit as a culinarian I was a bit sheepish about my kids riding up to school with a go-cup of cereal in tow because, you know, my reputation as a chef was on the line! But kids are kids and I always knew that Kevin and Jonathan would grow into enjoying real New Orleans breakfasts, lunches, and dinners soon enough. As a single father and chef, I know the importance of breakfast. Some days I'd be so desperate to get them to eat I'd resort to ice cream! I figured eggs, milk, carbs . . . okay, let's eat.

My boys were exposed to restaurant dining from a very early age. The boys always asked to look at the desert menu first. Confused waiters always asked for a gesture of approval from me, which I always gave. Kevin and Jonathan were planning their meals starting with the desert they could have if they finished their entrées. We negotiated this very early on and it was a big success that added a bit of fun. It was just our thing.

I am blessed to be making new memories with my ten-year-old son Noah. Being a father to Noah brings back a flood of happy times and memories of what it's like to have love and laughter permeating every corner of the house. Getting to raise Noah with two loving parents is simply a gift that I cherish. Noah's mom is a fantastic cook, but when I'm left to breakfast making, does the cereal in a Mardi Gras cup show up? Ice cream for breakfast? That might just have to be mine and Noah's little secret. And by the way, asking Noah if he is ordering dessert is like asking someone if they are going to catch beads at a Mardi Gras parade. Yes, indeed.

LAGNIAPPE

Louisiana's population of American alligator number around 2 million. These prehistoric behemoths flourish in the lakes and bayous around the state, and harvest season runs from August through September.

Alligator is best described as having a mild, light seafood flavor, and texture similar to pork. High protein and low in fat, the meat can be tough and is best cooked low and slow. Most of the meat from an alligator comes from the tail and the back strap. I've even dined on gator ribs—very memorable.

DUCK AND ANDOUILLE GUMBO WITH POTATO SALAD

I first saw Kevin's love of gumbo at Grandma Emily's in the 7th Ward. She always tempted him with gumbo. His eyes would light up and he would devour every drop put in front of him. The potato salad served on the side was her tradition that Kevin adopted and passed on to his children as the only way to eat gumbo. **Serves 8 to 10**

STOCK

2 whole ducks

5 quarts water

2 onions, peeled and quartered

4 stalks celery, cut in 2-inch sections

3 bay leaves

4 cloves garlic, smashed

1 teaspoon salt

1 teaspoon pepper

GUMBO

1 1/2 cups vegetable oil

1 1/2 cups all-purpose flour

2 cups chopped onion

1 cup chopped green bell pepper

1 cup chopped celery

3 bay leaves

1 1/2 tablespoons kosher salt

1 tablespoon pepper

2 tablespoons Creole seasoning

1 teaspoon cayenne pepper

10 cups duck stock

Reserved duck meat

1 1/2 pounds andouille sausage, cut in half lengthwise and sliced

STOCK

In a large stock pot, add the ducks, water, onions, celery, bay leaves, garlic, salt, and pepper. Turn stove on low to medium heat and simmer for 2 hours, or until ducks are tender. Remove ducks from the stock and pull the meat off of the bones; set aside. Reduce heat to low and continue simmering the stock for an additional 30 minutes. Remove from heat and cool. When cooled, skim the fat, strain the solids, and reserve stock for cooking.

GUMBO

In a large Dutch oven, heat the oil and gradually add the flour to form a roux, stirring continuously so not to burn. When the roux reaches the color of chocolate, add the onions and cook until transparent, about 5 minutes. Add bell pepper and celery and continue to cook in the roux until softened, about 4 minutes. Stir in the bay leaves, salt, pepper, seasoning, and cayenne.

Slowly add the stock, and stir in the duck meat and andouille. Bring to a boil, reduce heat, and simmer for 30-40 minutes.

POTaTO SalaD

Serves 8 to 10

5 large russet potatoes, peeled, cubed, and rinsed in cold water

1/2 cup finely chopped celery

1/2 cup finely chopped green onion

1 tablespoon minced fresh parsley

1 1/2 cups New Orleans-style mayonnaise

1 tablespoon yellow mustard

1 tablespoon Creole seasoning

4 eggs, boiled and chopped

Kosher salt and pepper, to taste

In a large pot, boil potatoes until soft, about 20 minutes. Remove from heat, drain, and let cool, about 20 minutes.

Place potatoes in a large bowl. Add the celery, onion, and parsley and gently mix to combine. Slowly add mayonnaise 1/2 cup at a time, until you reach the desired consistency. Add mustard, seasoning, and chopped eggs. Mix well but do not overmix. You want the potatoes to hold their shape. Adjust seasoning with salt and pepper. Chill in the refrigerator for 2 hours or overnight before serving.

TIPS & SUggestiONS

If you cannot find andouille, any firm (not fresh) smoked sausage works with the flavor profile you are looking to achieve.

NoaH's steak au Poivre

Noah's love of meat has kept my seafood palate honest. I revisited how to cook a good steak with New Orleans flair thanks to Noah. It starts with a hot, hot cast iron skillet and simple seasoning, with pepper being tops for him. Crust on the outside, medium on the inside, and finished with butter and other ingredients to make a sauce—because you know we love our sauces down here. **Serves 4**

---

4 (6-ounce) filet mignon steaks

1 tablespoon kosher salt

2 teaspoons whole black peppercorns

1 teaspoon vegetable oil

1/3 cup finely chopped shallots

4 tablespoons unsalted butter, cubed and divided

1/2 cup cognac

3/4 cup heavy cream

1 teaspoon Creole seasoning

1 tablespoon Creole mustard

1 tablespoon chopped fresh parsley

Preheat oven to 200 degrees. Rinse steaks, and thoroughly pat dry. Season with salt.

Place peppercorns in a sealed plastic bag, wrap with a kitchen towel, and crush with the bottom of a heavy skillet or meat mallet. Poivre (pepper) the filets by pressing the crushed peppercorns evenly on both sides of steaks.

Heat a heavy cast iron skillet over medium heat until extremely hot, about 3 minutes. Add oil and coat the bottom of the hot skillet thoroughly. Return to heat and wait until the pan is lightly smoking, about 30 seconds. Sear steaks, 2 at a time, about 6-7 minutes on each side for medium rare. Remove from heat, place on an ovenproof platter, and hold in oven to keep warm.

Pour off fat from skillet, leaving the debris and peppercorns behind. Return skillet to medium-low heat, add the shallots, 2 tablespoons of butter, and sauté until shallots are translucent, scraping the bottom of the skillet while cooking. Once shallots are browned, 3-5 minutes, add cognac (use caution as it may flame, but will burn off once alcohol evaporates), stirring as it reduces to a thin glaze, about 3 minutes. Add cream, Creole seasoning, mustard, parsley, and any meat juices from resting meat platter. Bring to a boil and reduce by half, about 3 minutes. Whisk in remaining butter and serve hot over steaks.

TIPS & suggestions

If you prefer your steak with a bit of fat marbling, a New York strip, rib-eye, or porterhouse cut is perfectly acceptable. The fat from those cuts will yield a base for a pan sauce.

Alligator Sauce Piquant

No culture in the United States relates to alligator as a food source or mascot more than we do here in New Orleans. My son Jonathan loves this dish and the flavors that the tomato and extra seasoning impart to elevate the gator meat to pure deliciousness. Piquant style works for any game dish, and we owe the technique to our Cajun cousins. It's my belief that Jonathan not only loves it for the taste, but because it truly is one of the most unique dishes from New Orleans. **Serves 6**

---

1 cup vegetable oil

1 cup all-purpose flour

2 cups chopped onion

1 cup chopped celery

1/2 cup chopped green bell pepper

1 tablespoon chopped garlic

2 tablespoons all-purpose seasoning

1 pound alligator meat, cubed

1 teaspoon salt

1/8 cup tomato paste

4 to 5 cups chicken stock

4 bay leaves

1/4 teaspoon white pepper

1/2 cup chopped fresh parsley

2 cups hot cooked rice

In a large skillet, heat oil and stir in flour to make a roux, cooking flour to a dark peanut butter color. Add onion, celery, and bell pepper; sauté for 5 minutes. Add garlic, seasoning, and alligator and sauté for 3 minutes. Add salt, tomato paste, stock, bay leaves, and pepper. Stir well and simmer for 30-40 minutes, covered. Stir occasionally. Add parsley and serve over rice.

TIPS & SUGGESTIONS

Admittedly, alligator might be difficult to find in your local grocery store. Some other meat options for a sauce piquant include rabbit, redfish, chicken, and duck. Use what's easy to source, and come to New Orleans for the alligator.

coffee, stock, and brown sugar. Stir thoroughly and reduce until thickened, about 7 minutes. Serve with the roast and vegetables.

TIP & SUGGESTIONS

For my big coffee fans, simply eliminate the beef broth and go all coffee for a more intense flavor.

BBQ BaBY BaCK RIBS WITH a SWeeT COFFee RUB

Many years ago my good friend Chef Michael Ruoss, an annual competitor in the New Orleans-based Hogs for a Cause barbecue competition and fundraising event, served me a batch of ribs he made for his daughter's birthday. Those ribs were the most perfect ribs I have ever eaten. Every time I cook ribs, my goal is to make them like Mike's. **Serves 4**

SWeeT COFFee BBQ RUB

1/4 cup medium-roast, finely ground coffee

1/4 cup brown sugar

2 tablespoons chili powder

2 tablespoons kosher salt

1 tablespoon freshly cracked pepper

1 tablespoon smoked paprika

1 tablespoon garlic powder

1 tablespoon onion powder

1 tablespoon Creole seasoning

BaBY BaCK RIBS

1 rack baby back ribs

1/2 cup strong coffee

1/2 cup beef stock

3 tablespoons Creole mustard

3 tablespoons brown sugar

SWeeT COFFee BBQ RUB

In a small mixing bowl combine the coffee, sugar, and spices. This can be stored up to 2 months in a sealed jar.

BaBY BaCK RIBS

Prepare the ribs by removing fat cap along back of ribs; rinse and pat dry. Cut into 3 sections to prepare for using a pressure cooker.

Thoroughly coat ribs on all sides with the dry rub. Set on a tray, cover with plastic wrap, and refrigerate for at least 4 hours and up to 24 hours.

Combine the coffee and stock in the pressure cooker. Place the steamer insert inside the cooker and lay the seasoned ribs on the insert. Following the manufacturer's directions, carefully lock the lid in place and bring the cooker to high pressure. Maintain the pressure for 20 minutes for tender ribs and up to 30 minutes to achieve fall-off-the-bone doneness.

Turn cooker to the off position and let the pressure fall before unlocking the lid. Remove the ribs using tongs and transfer to a lined platter. As the liquid in the cooker cools, the fat will rise to the top. Skim fat off and discard.

Preheat oven on broiler setting.

Transfer the liquid to a saucepan, bring to a boil, and reduce by 1/3. Add mustard and brown sugar and simmer for 5 minutes, or until sauce is a thick syrup.

Baste ribs with thickened sauce and place in oven for 4 minutes, or until sauce is bubbling. Remove from oven, turn ribs, baste, and return to oven for another 4 minutes, or until sauce is bubbling. Remove and serve.

TIP & SUGGESTIONS

Prefer beef ribs? No problem. They work great in this recipe, too. Depending on the size of your pressure cooker, make sure the ribs you purchase will fit in the cooker. You can ask your butcher to cut them to your preferred size.

NO-CHURN COFFEE ICE CREAM

"Do you want ice cream?" Ask any kid, and the usual answer is "Yes!" I fell for it every time my parents asked. I forgot about the churn. But, before I had a chance to change my mind, Mom was cooking the custard and I was committed to an hour of handle turning. I remember the wooden bucket, metal insert, and the iron churn handle. I'd sit on the front porch, and every few minutes Mom would come and check to make sure I was turning and churning. Right arm. Switch to left arm. Before long, I was rewarded with the fruits of my labor—the most delicious homemade ice cream on this earth. A testimony to my culinary commitment at an early age. This recipe takes the work out of making the ice cream, but the reward is still there. **Serves 10 to 12**

---

1 pint heavy whipping cream

1 teaspoon vanilla

$^1/_2$ teaspoon salt

2 tablespoons instant coffee

2 tablespoons water

14 ounces sweetened condensed milk

Line a large bread pan with parchment paper; set aside.

In a mixing bowl, whip the cream until soft peaks form. Fold in the vanilla and salt, and continue to beat until the mixture holds stiff peaks, about 30 seconds more.

In a small bowl, mix the instant coffee with the water, add the condensed milk and stir well. Pour on top of the cream and fold in gently.

Carefully pour the ice cream into the bread pan. Freeze for at least 12 hours before serving.

TIPS & SUGGESTIONS

Crumble your favorite cookie and fold in for added texture and flavor. Mini chocolate chips work great and are light enough to float through the ice cream unlike the larger ones that tend to sink to the bottom.

PO' BOYS

My mother made my first po' boy. It was a fried shrimp po' boy, and I can still taste it today. Momma would get her loaves of French bread from the Leidenheimer Baking Company. Most probably she'd have Dad pick them up fresh from the bakery, and then it was po' boy making time.

Nan and I would peel the shrimp. Mom would season her fish fry and heat up her cast iron skillet filled with oil so once our work was done she could fry the fresh fat shrimp just how she liked them. She'd slice those huge bread loaves down the middle and slather Blue Plate mayonnaise on the top slice and butter on the bottom slice. She'd layer pickles on the mayo, and then she would carefully layer a few slices of fresh tomatoes, Creole tomatoes if they were in season, on the buttered side. Then she would pile up the shrimp and sprinkle hot sauce on top.

The next step was a furious chop of iceberg lettuce, and she would sprinkle that on the shrimp side. With a flourish she quickly folded over the two halves, and in one swift motion sliced off a huge portion and plopped in onto a plate right in front of me. That's how she did the shrimp po' boy.

Her oyster po' boy came together a little differently. She would butter the French bread on both sides. Then she would load one side up with pickles. She would add a generous sprinkle of hot sauce, and then her crispy fried oysters were placed right on top of the loaf. Fresh fried? Yes. Less than a minute out of the cast iron skillet. She always told me never put lettuce and tomato on the oyster po' boy because they mask the oyster flavor. She got that tradition from Lavata's in the 7th Ward. The only two places I've ever had an oyster po' boy was either at Lavata's or at home. And as much as I loved Lavata's—there's no place like home.

LAGNIAPPE

Clovis and Bennie Martin invented the poor boy sandwich in the 2000 block of St. Claude Avenue at their Martin Bros. restaurant at the corner of Touro and St. Claude. These former streetcar drivers, long given up on their driving days by the early 1920s, created this cheap meal to cater to the picketers in the 1929 streetcar strike. The term "poor boys" was possibly in response to the unfair treatment and low wages offered to their comrades, or simply because being on strike meant no pay and empty pockets, making one a true poor boy. Poor boy is pronounced po' boy in Louisiana lingo.

SLOW-COOKED ROAST BEEF PO' BOY

Aficionados of New Orleans-style po' boys understand that the roast version is the "one that came first." Those who get hooked on this tasty combination become adamant over who serves the best. Not only is taste vital, but some also note the importance of how many napkins you use while eating a juicy and gravy laden po' boy. For real. Anything less than five napkins won't do. **Serves 8**

---

1 (3- to 4-pound) rump roast

1 teaspoon salt

1 teaspoon pepper

1 teaspoon minced garlic

12 ounces root beer

2 loaves French bread

Butter, room temperature

8 tablespoons Homemade Creole Mayonnaise

32 slices dill pickles

24 slices tomato

1 head iceberg lettuce, shredded

Prepare meat by rinsing then rubbing with salt, pepper, and garlic. Pour root beer in bottom of slow cooker and add the meat. Cover and cook on medium for 8-10 hours, or until meat is cooked and falling apart.

To make the po' boys, cut the bread into 8 equal servings and slice in half lengthwise. Coat the bread slices with a thin spread of butter then layer mayonnaise on both sides, using 1 tablespoon per sandwich. Add meat to the sandwiches and top each with 4 pickle slices, 3 tomato slices, and a pile of lettuce.

TIPS & SUGGESTIONS

Mayonnaise is traditional but mustard is delicious, too. We like Creole mustard for the zest of the flavor. Use what you love.

HOMEMADE CREOLE MAYONNAISE

Makes 1/2 cup

1/2 cup mayonnaise

1 1/2 teaspoons Creole mustard

1 teaspoon Creole seasoning

2 cloves garlic, smashed and chopped to paste consistency

1/8 teaspoon coarse pepper

1/2 teaspoon fresh lemon juice

Dash hot sauce

Dash Worcestershire sauce

In a small bowl, thoroughly combine all ingredients. Cover and chill in refrigerator for 30 minutes. Will keep in refrigerator for up to two weeks in a covered container.

Fried Oyster Po' Boy with Blue Cheese Buffalo Sauce

I distinctly remember going with Mom to buy oysters and thinking how can something with such a soft texture turn into a crispy, delightful morsel when fried. I recall perfectly the taste of my first fried oyster from Momma's kitchen. I was sold. The fried "oyster loaf" of my youth was topped with pickles and hot sauce. This version pairs the oysters with my love of blue cheese and spiciness. The flavors meld perfectly, and shows that you can be authentic and creative with the versatile po' boy. **Serves 4**

Vegetable oil

3 dozen oysters in brine, drained

1 1/2 cups whole milk

2 1/2 cups fine yellow cornmeal

2 cups all-purpose flour

2 tablespoons Creole seasoning

1 teaspoon kosher salt

1 loaf French bread, sliced in half lengthwise

Sliced tomatoes, optional

Shredded lettuce, optional

Blue Cheese Buffalo Sauce

1/3 cup hot sauce

3 tablespoons butter, melted

1/3 cup crumbled blue cheese

2 tablespoons finely chopped green onion

Heat oil to 375 degrees in a large cast iron skillet.

Place the oysters in a bowl and cover with milk; set aside.

Combine the cornmeal, flour, Creole seasoning, and salt in a mixing bowl. Remove the oysters 1 at a time from the milk, allowing enough of the milk to drip off so that the oysters are damp but not overly wet. Roll each oyster in the cornmeal mixture to thoroughly coat, patting the coating in to cover completely. Place on wax paper and continue to coat until all the oysters are ready to fry.

Place 6-8 oysters in the hot oil, being careful not to overfill, and fry until the sides curl and they turn golden, about 1 1/2 minutes. Remove and place on a paper towel to drain.

Blue Cheese Buffalo Sauce

Place the hot sauce, butter, cheese, and onion in a small bowl and combine well.

To serve, place oysters on 1 side of the bread. Drizzle Blue Cheese Buffalo Sauce over oysters and dress the other side of the bread with lettuce and tomatoes, if you wish. Fold the 2 sides of bread together, slice into servings, and serve warm.

Tips & Suggestions

For a "closer walk with thee," add bacon.

French Fry Po' Boy with Gravy

I love potatoes. French fry perfection for me is a hand-cut wedge, fried crisp on the outside, and soft and hot on the inside. The only way to make this happen is using my twice fry technique. By the way, the French fry po' boy is not some abstract, esoteric concoction. It appears on most po' boy shop menus. It may seem unusual, but around New Orleans it's well known. And for the record, this is as close to vegetarian as I get. **Serves 4**

Gravy

6 slices bacon

3 tablespoons bacon grease

1/4 cup all-purpose flour

2 cups whole milk

Salt and pepper, to taste

The Perfect French Fries

3 large russet potatoes, rinsed and scrubbed

Ice water

Vegetable oil

1 loaf French bread

Gravy

In a large cast iron skillet, fry bacon on medium-high heat until crisp, about 10 minutes. Remove bacon and place on a paper towel to drain. Reserve 3 tablespoons of grease in pan and store rest for use later.

In a small bowl, slowly whisk the flour into the milk to prevent lumps. When fully incorporated, slowly begin to add flour mixture back to skillet over medium heat. Stir continuously so not to burn, heating until bubbling and thick, about 10 minutes. Stir in salt and pepper. Crumble the bacon and add to the gravy.

The Perfect French Fries

Cut potatoes into pieces about 1/4-3/8 inch thick and about 4 inches in length. As you cut the potatoes, drop them into a bowl with the ice water. Drain and pat dry.

Heat oil to 350 degrees in deep fryer.

Fry potatoes in small batches for about 2 minutes per batch. Remove and drain on paper towels.

Once all the potatoes have had their first fry, here is where the magic happens. Heat oil back up to 350 degrees and fry potatoes in small batches for about 3 minutes, or until they start to turn golden brown, allowing the temperature of the oil to recover after each fry. Remove and drain on paper towels. Once drained, lightly salt the fries.

To assemble your po' boys, cut the bread into 4 sandwich-size pieces and then slice each piece almost in half, being careful not to cut all the way through. Top each sandwich with a generous helping of fries then smother with gravy.

Tips & Suggestions

Salt or season your fries immediately after removing from the oil and draining them to ensure the seasoning sticks. That's where you get the flavors to come together.

SPRING IN NEW ORLEANS

New Orleans has two seasons—summer and the rest of the year. Makes me laugh when I think about it. Almost everyone around the world can relate to the four seasons, but I have to really think about it because I don't match holidays and events with the time of the year. It's more like I try to recall events and the food we ate. I picture what the inside of our house looked like. And by that, I mean "Did Mom have the heavy drapes up or the light lacy curtains?" I really do keep this visual in my head and I'll explain why.

A change in season at the Belton house meant Mom would change the drapes. In some households, rugs would get rolled up for summer, and maybe a different throw or couch cover would be draped across the sofa. But at our house, warmer temperatures meant light lacy curtains. It gets hot and humid in a New Orleans summer. The rest of the year is delightful except for the four or five days around Mardi Gras that just might get "freezing" cold. And that means maybe 40 degrees. When the thermometer drops below that, all of us scramble for a scarf and heavy jacket. Usually searching for that jacket takes a lot of time. They are stored way back in the closet and we pull them out only once or twice a year. But let me put that in context. We aren't having 20-degree weather. We pull out the coats when it hits 59.9 degrees. It's a hoot.

Besides the drapes, Mom changed the menu. Everything she made once the weather warmed up was a bit lighter. In the spring (that's when the menu started to transition) Mom still served some hearty foods that were cooked in the oven, but she introduced a few important dishes that reminded us summer was coming. The recipes in this chapter reflect that transition tradition.

LAGNIAPPE

Boudin, pronounced "Boo-dan" not "Bow-DIN," is a fresh sausage and staple food in the Cajun country of Southwest Louisiana. It's a cooked amalgamation of fresh meat, usually beef or pork, with rice and a secret combination of spices. It's this boudin meat that is stuffed in a casing or used to make patties or little meatball-size balls for frying. And it is so much a part of daily life in the southwestern part of the state that there is actually a directory of more than 100 grocery stores, mini-marts, and restaurants that serve up their own style of boudin along the Southwest Louisiana Boudin Trail.

ASParagus SouP

I love the sharp flavor of asparagus. I can eat asparagus raw, cooked, or any other way that comes up. I do love this soup. I especially enjoy how the roux and the milk soften the sharp edge and become a flavor that converts people who formerly were not into the delicious green spears. **Serves 4**

---

1 pound asparagus, trimmed and cut into 1-inch pieces

1/2 cup finely chopped white onion

2 cups chicken stock, divided

1/2 pound mirliton (chayote), peeled and chopped

2 tablespoons unsalted butter

2 tablespoons all-purpose flour

1 teaspoon Creole seasoning

1 teaspoon kosher salt

1 cup whole milk

Sour cream, optional

Lemon wedges, optional

Crackers, optional

In a large saucepan, combine asparagus, onion, 1 cup broth, and mirliton. Bring to a boil, reduce heat, and simmer, uncovered, until asparagus and mirliton are tender, about 15 minutes. Purée soup with a hand-held immersion blender in the pot until smooth, or in small batches in a blender until creamy (use caution blending hot liquids). Set aside.

Using same saucepan, melt butter over medium-low heat. Stir in flour to make a light roux. Add Creole seasoning and salt and stir to incorporate. Slowly add remaining stock and continue to stir. Increase to medium heat. Continue to whisk until mixture comes to a boil, about 4 minutes. Add asparagus mixture and milk and continue to cook until soup thickens, about 7 minutes.

To serve, garnish with a dollop of sour cream, lemon wedges on the side, or a cracker.

TIPS & SUGGESTIONS

White asparagus has the same flavor profile as the green, and works well in this recipe. I like to add fresh crabmeat as a garnish.

ROASTED ROOT VEGETABLES MARINATED IN WINE AND COFFEE

*I particularly like the heartiness of a root vegetable. The dry wine and coffee combination enhances what I describe as the earth notes of the flavors. Simply roasting after marinating creates flavors that can be an entire meal unto itself. I think of this as a perfect dish for a chilly night's dinner. We don't have many chilly nights in New Orleans, but I'm not going to let that stop me. Just crank up the air conditioner and pretend. If there are any leftovers, chill overnight. These veggies are delicious the next day for a perfect light lunch. **Serves 8***

---

1 pound unpeeled carrots, with tops, cut on diagonal,

2 large red beets, cut in quarters, with tops

2 large golden beets, cut in quarters, with tops

2 large onions, peeled, cut in quarters

2 large potatoes, cut in 2-inch cubes

1 whole garlic bulb, top sliced off

1 cup medium-roast whole coffee beans

2 tablespoons cumin seeds

1 tablespoon red, black, and white whole peppercorns

1 tablespoon fennel seeds

2 tablespoons whole coriander

2 tablespoons Himalayan salt

$1/3$ cup extra virgin olive oil

$1/8$ cup dry white wine

Preheat oven to 375 degrees.

Place the prepared vegetables and garlic in a large, ovenproof baking pan.

In a small bowl, combine the coffee beans and spices with the olive oil and wine. Mix thoroughly. Drizzle marinade over vegetables and toss to coat. Bake for 1 hour, stirring after 30 minutes. Vegetables are done when tender and can easily be pierced with a knife.

TIPS & SUGGESTIONS

Broccoli, asparagus, and cauliflower all make excellent additions to this roasting technique. Be aware of roasting times for each vegetable and add separately throughout the roasting process. For example, asparagus only needs 20 minutes to roast. So add it to the pan for the last 20 minutes of roasting time. Be sure to spoon some of the marinade over the vegetables when you add them to the pan.

ROaST DUCK QUarTers WITH HOney-BOUrBON Gravy anD BOUDIn SQuares

Instead of cooking a whole duck, I prefer to cut the duck into pieces. This helps the fat to render out, and the duck cooks in a shorter amount of time, allowing the meat to fully develop flavor. The pan gravy with the addition of bourbon alongside the honey adds a touch of sweet oakiness, allowing for a gravy full of character. The savory boudin square crumbles into the gravy for another simple but complex pairing. **Serves 4**

DUCK

2 duck breast and leg quarters, with skin

1 tablespoon vegetable oil

1 teaspoon salt

HOney-BOUrBON Gravy

3 tablespoons duck fat

Butter, if needed

3 tablespoons all-purpose flour

1/3 cup bourbon

1/2 cup duck or chicken stock, plus more if needed

2 tablespoons honey

2 teaspoons Creole seasoning

1 teaspoon hot sauce

2 tablespoons heavy cream

BOUDIN SQuares

4 cups crumbled cornbread

1 day-old French baguette, chopped

1 cup unsalted chicken stock, divided

3 tablespoons vegetable oil

3 links boudin, casings removed

1 1/2 cups chopped celery

1/2 cup chopped green bell pepper

1 cup chopped yellow onion

1 clove garlic, minced

3 teaspoons Creole seasoning

1 teaspoon kosher salt

1/8 teaspoon cayenne pepper

2 eggs, whisked

DUCK

Preheat oven to 425 degrees.

Score duck breasts and thoroughly coat each piece with oil and season with salt. Place in a cast iron baking pan that is large enough to hold both pieces without them touching.

Roast for about 20 minutes, or until duck reaches an internal temperature of 135-140 degrees.

Remove from oven and place pan on stovetop. Remove duck and place on a cutting board to rest. Turn heat to medium high. Place duck breasts back in pan, skin side down, and sear until skin crisps,

Continued

3-4 minutes. Remove from pan and place back on cutting board.

Honey-Bourbon Gravy

To make the gravy, leave about 3 tablespoons of duck fat in bottom of pan. Add butter if you need more volume. Sprinkle in the flour and stir for about 5 minutes until the flour and fat begins to turn a light brown. Add the bourbon carefully in case it flames over the heat. Immediately add stock, stirring constantly. Reduce heat to a simmer. Add honey, Creole seasoning, and hot sauce. Stir and check consistency. Adjust with stock if needed. Add cream, stir, and cook for 1 minute. Remove from heat.

Boudin Squares

Preheat oven to 325 degrees.

Combine cornbread and baguette pieces in a large bowl. Add $1/8$ cup chicken stock and toss to moisten.

In a large skillet over medium-high heat, add oil and sauté boudin (boudin will crumble while cooking), celery, bell pepper, and onion until translucent, about 5 minutes. Add garlic and cook until you can smell it, about 1 minute. Add Creole seasoning, salt, and cayenne and continue to cook for another minute. Transfer to bread mixture and mix thoroughly. Add egg and remaining stock; mix until well-combined.

Transfer to a greased baking dish and pat evenly into the bottom. Bake for 45 minutes, or until done. Slice into squares and serve with duck meat and gravy.

Tips & Suggestions

I've done this recipe with chicken and pork chops instead of duck. Delicious.

ST. JOSEPH'S DAY

I wore khaki pants, a khaki shirt, black socks and black shoes to school. It was my uniform for 12 years. And for anyone who lives or visits New Orleans, you are quick to note this is the uniform of a Catholic School student. I am a proud graduate of Our Lady of Lourdes at the corner of Napoleon Avenue and Freret Street. I graduated high school from Brother Martin in Gentilly. Catholic education was very important to both sides of the family, and I loved it.

I can remember being in first grade and learning about the "cool" saints. We prayed to all of them. St. Christopher protects you when you travel. St. Blaise was super fun because once a year we would hang out after daily morning mass to have Monsieur Strassel place crossed candles and bless us in the name of St. Blaise. That was so we would not get as many sore throats. And, Grandma Emily first introduced me to St. Jude. She was a big fan. St. Jude is the one who helps out when you lose something. I'm notorious for dialing him in because I do lose my keys.

As a Catholic school kid, March marked our yearly visits to local St. Joseph altars led by the nuns and teachers. I have to say that as an adult, I truly appreciate the hard work and camaraderie of the ladies who constructed these phenomenal displays of devotion and food. Which leads me to explain the viewing of these altars was pure torture to my childhood self. And by that I mean we were never offered any of the food. You walked in front of and around the altars and you heard nothing because all you saw were cakes, cookies, and other elaborate foods. At the end of the tour, they handed you this weird, hard bean called a fava bean and they'd say, "That's for good luck." I used to think if that bean was lucky, surely one of those Italian ladies would trade it for a cookie.

I've viewed hundreds of altars over the years. To this day I'm waiting for an invitation to attend the dismantling of a St. Joseph's altar. I'll be there if invited. I've saved that fava bean to trade for a cookie.

LAGNIAPPE

Walk through any neighborhood in New Orleans and you will see fig trees lining the sidewalks and peeking over backyard fences. Figs trees love the heat and humidity and thrive in New Orleans. It's noted that the first fig trees appeared in Louisiana in the sixteenth century.

Eaten fresh, the flavor is delicate and textural. Dried, they intensify in sweetness and density. Figs are the perfect base for jams and jellies. It takes 3–4 years for a fig tree to begin producing. But once established, they produce abundantly.

Fried Artichokes with Mudrica

Mudrica, which represents the sawdust in homage to St. Joseph being a carpenter, is traditionally served over pasta. I wanted to do something a little different and took the idea of the popular stuffed artichoke, and combined that with this traditional St. Joseph's Day altar element. **Serves 4**

---

2 cups vegetable oil

2 eggs

$1/2$ cup whole milk

1 (15-ounce) can artichoke hearts, drained and quartered

$1 1/2$ cups Italian-seasoned breadcrumbs

$1/2$ cup Mudrica

Heat oil to 350 degrees in deep fryer or cast iron skillet. In a small bowl, whisk eggs and milk together. Dip artichoke hearts in egg mixture and roll in breadcrumbs to coat. Gently drop breaded artichokes into hot oil in batches, being careful not to overcrowd fryer. Cook until lightly golden, about 2 minutes; remove and drain on paper towels. Sprinkle with Mudrica and enjoy.

TIPS & Suggestions

For best results, only use artichoke hearts packed in their own liquid.

Mudrica

Makes $3/4$ cup

$1/2$ cup plain breadcrumbs

$1/8$ cup olive oil

4 tablespoons grated Parmesan cheese

2 tablespoons toasted pine nuts

2 tablespoons dried currants or raisins

1 teaspoon crushed red pepper

$1/4$ teaspoon ground cinnamon

$1/8$ teaspoon chopped fresh oregano leaves

Pinch kosher salt

Place all the ingredients in a food processor and pulse until fully blended. The mixture should be slightly dry.

Mudrica can be stored in an air tight container for up to 2 weeks for later use.

crawfish Bread

I call this Louisiana pizza. It's super easy to make, and fast. It will keep your crowd at bay while dinner is in the works. The quintessential crawfish bread is the Panorama Foods version served at The Jazz and Heritage Festival to rave reviews. Follow this recipe and you can get your fix in between festivals. **Serves 6 to 8**

---

1 baguette or loaf French bread

1/2 cup mayonnaise

2 tablespoons butter

3/4 cup finely chopped Vidalia onion

2 cloves garlic, minced

1 pound cooked crawfish tails

3/4 cup chopped green onion

1 tablespoon chopped fresh parsley

1 teaspoon Creole seasoning

8 ounces cream cheese, softened

1/2 cup grated Parmesan cheese

3/4 cup grated Monterey jack cheese

1/2 teaspoon sweet paprika

Chopped fresh parsley, to garnish

Preheat oven to 375 degrees.

Slice the bread in half lengthwise and place on a baking sheet. Coat halves evenly with mayonnaise.

In a large skillet over medium heat, melt the butter and sauté onion until translucent, about 5 minutes. Add garlic and cook until it releases aroma, about 1 minute. Add crawfish, green onion, and parsley, and cook until heated through, 4–5 minutes. Add Creole seasoning and stir. Add cream cheese, remove from heat, and continue to stir until cheese is melted.

Divide mixture and spread evenly over both bread halves. Top with cheeses and sprinkle with paprika. Bake for about 15 minutes. Turn oven to broil and broil close to flame or heat until cheese has browned, 1-2 minutes. Serve warm.

TIPS & SUGGESTIONS

You can easily substitute cooked shrimp, chopped into bite-size pieces, or shredded chicken for the crawfish in this recipe.

ITALIAN FIG COOKIES

There are fig trees growing everywhere in New Orleans. All of my parents' neighbors had fig trees. And today, most of my friends have them in their yards. Every July we harvest unbelievable amounts of figs from trees that need very little care. We usually have more figs than we can eat, so fig preserves line the pantry shelves.

With its prominence in religion as well as being grown in Louisiana, it is fitting that the fig takes a hallowed place on St. Joseph Day altars. **Makes 48 to 60 cookies**

FILLING

1 cup packed dried figs, hard tops discarded

3/4 cup raisins

3/4 cup honey

1/4 cup brandy

1 1/2 teaspoons finely grated orange zest

1 teaspoon finely grated lemon zest

1 tablespoon ground cinnamon

1/4 teaspoon ground cloves

1/4 teaspoon freshly grated nutmeg

3/4 cup toasted, coarsely chopped whole almonds

3/4 cup toasted, coarsely chopped walnuts

PASTRY DOUGH

4 cups all-purpose flour

1 cup plus 2 tablespoons sugar

1 tablespoon baking powder

1 teaspoon salt

1 cup cold salted butter, cut into 1/2-inch cubes

2 eggs, lightly beaten

1/2 cup whole milk

1 1/2 teaspoons vanilla

1 teaspoon finely grated orange or lemon zest

ICING

1 cup powdered sugar

1/2 teaspoon vanilla

1 1/2 to 2 tablespoons fresh orange juice

Multicolored nonpareil, optional

FILLING

Pulse figs and raisins in a food processor until finely chopped. Place in a bowl and stir in remaining filling ingredients until well-combined. Cover and chill in refrigerator for at least 8 hours.

PASTRY DOUGH

Whisk together flour, sugar, baking powder, and salt in a large bowl. Add butter and rub into the flour with your fingertips or cut in with a pastry blender (or pulse in a food processor) until mixture resembles coarse meal roughly the size of peas. Add eggs, milk, vanilla, and zest and stir with a fork until a soft dough forms. Divide the dough

in 2 equal pieces and gather each half into a ball. Flatten each ball into a rough 4 x 6-inch rectangle between sheets of plastic wrap. Place in refrigerator and chill until firm, for at least 8 hours.

Preheat oven to 350 degrees.

Remove 1 piece of dough from the refrigerator and roll into a 14 x 15-inch rectangle on a well-floured surface with a floured rolling pin. Trim to a 10 x 13-inch rectangle; reserve and chill trimmings, then cut into 4 (3 $1/4$ x 10-inch) strips. Arrange $1/3$ cup of filling in a 1-inch-wide log down the center of each strip then fold sides of each strip up over filling, pinching edges together to seal. Turn rolls seam-side down and press gently to flatten seams. Cut logs crosswise with a floured knife into 1 $1/2$-inch-wide slices and arrange $1/2$ inch apart on large buttered baking sheets. Repeat with remaining chilled dough, trimmings (reroll once), and filling.

Bake cookies in batches in middle of oven until golden around edges, 16-20 minutes. Transfer cookies to wire racks and cool until warm, about 10 minutes.

ICING

Whisk together powdered sugar, vanilla, and enough orange juice to make a pourable icing. Brush icing on warm cookies and decorate with nonpareils then cool completely.

TIPS & SUGGESTIONS

For those with nut allergies, leave out the almonds and walnuts. You get the same results—a great tasting cookie.

Filling can be made 1 week ahead and chilled, covered. Dough can be chilled, wrapped in plastic wrap and then foil, and stored for up to 3 days. Cookies keep, layered between sheets of wax paper or parchment paper, in an airtight container at room temperature for up to 1 week.

Decatur Street Olive Salad

Olive salad is the star of the New Orleans muffuletta sandwich. But that's not the only use for this beloved olive-based dish. I love to use it as a topping for a salad. Sometimes, I toss the olive salad with cooked pasta and chill for a snack or luncheon dish, top toast points as a quick appetizer, or use as a topping for grilled fish. **Serves 4**

3/4 cup chopped whole black and green olives, in oil

1 tablespoon capers

1/4 cup chopped roasted red peppers

2 tablespoons chopped parsley

1/2 cup chopped giardiniera

1 teaspoon minced garlic

1 tablespoon red wine vinegar

3 tablespoons extra virgin olive oil

Combine the olives, capers, red peppers, parsley, giardiniera, and garlic in a food processor and pulse until the mixture has no pieces larger than 1/2 inch. Transfer to a glass or non-reactive bowl and toss with vinegar and oil. Cover and refrigerate overnight so the salad develops flavor.

TIPS & SUGGESTIONS

This can last up to 3 weeks in a sealed container in the refrigerator. It's great just to keep on hand for a quick addition to a meal or snack.

SERIOUSLY GOOD SHELLFISH

Peeling a cooked shrimp is way different than peeling a fresh shrimp. I learned how to do both at a very early age thanks to my Grandma Nan. Nan was Mom's sous chef for every meal. I was Nan's intern. She knew how to peel a shrimp and crack a crab with more finesse and speed than I've ever seen since. Fresh or cooked, to this day I'd put her up against any of the pros I've worked with over the years. And that's saying a lot.

I think it was those times spent with Nan prepping shrimp or crabs that Uncle Chet or Dad brought home kept us close and made me think of her as my best friend. 'Cause hanging in the kitchen, chatting, and making food, that's what you do here in New Orleans. You make meals together and make memories.

I love it when I arrive early to a party or a dinner and I get to help out in the kitchen or in the backyard or driveway if I'm at a crawfish boil. You learn other techniques or tricks you wouldn't find out about otherwise. It's those times that you get to appreciate how much fun it is to hang out in New Orleans.

LAGNIAPPE

Mudbugs. Crayfish. Mini Lobster. Craw Daddies. And, of course, crawfish. These freshwater crustaceans thrive in Southwest Louisiana, particularly in the tributaries and estuaries of the Atchafalaya Basin. That's Cajun country. Louisiana towns with names like Houma, Des Allemandes, Breaux Bridge, and Pierre Part are ground zero for one of the most unique ingredients of Louisiana cooking.

Crawfish are purchased alive and are easily transported in an insulated cooler. You gotta prop the lid open a bit to keep the oxygen flowing and sprinkle with water to keep them moist. I drop the entire sack in to keep them maintained. Otherwise, and trust me from experience, you'll have 200 crawfish running all over the back seat of your car.

For the iconic crawfish boil, we purchase a sack or two of live crawfish. Sacks come in red, green, and purple. The color of the sack is a code that means a whole lot. A red sack contains premiums, or what I call "super-fat big-daddy crawfish," about 18 crawfish to a pound. The green sacks are select grade crawfish that are a mix of medium and large, and are referred to as restaurant packs for the fact that this size has become the go-to for culinarians. Peelers come in a purple sack labeled quality grade and are not normally purchased for a boil because they are so small. However, the smallest are perfect for boiling, peeling, and freezing for later when you crave them and the season is long over.

TRADITIONAL SEAFOOD BOIL

The local newspaper lining makeshift tables in the yard or driveway is one of the hallmarks of a Louisiana boil. In the spring we start collecting copies of the newspapers to make sure we had enough to paper our serving table. Of course a boil isn't just for two or three people. Announce a boil and expect neighbors, cousins, and your friends to show. Pour a huge steaming pot of crawfish or shrimp with the corn and potatoes on top of the newsprint and you can expect lots of conversation and laughter as everyone works away at the bounty. You've gotta work hard to peel and eat the crawfish, but nobody minds. It's part of the culture. **Serves 8**

---

12 whole cloves

$1/4$ cup coriander seeds

$1/4$ cup mustard seeds

3 tablespoons dill seeds

1 tablespoon celery seeds

1 tablespoon red pepper flakes

2 tablespoons whole allspice

2 tablespoons black peppercorns

6 whole bay leaves, crumbled

Cheese cloth and kitchen string

16 quarts water, divided

$1/3$ cup canola oil

6 yellow onions, unpeeled

4 stalks celery, halved

2 lemons, cut in quarters

12 cloves garlic

5 whole bay leaves

1 (2-inch) piece fresh ginger, peeled and sliced thick

$1/2$ cup sea salt

1 tablespoon Creole seasoning

$2 1/2$ pounds small red potatoes, cut in half

6 ears fresh yellow corn, split in fourths

5 pounds shrimp (16/20 size), with heads and shells

In a bowl, mix together cloves, coriander seeds, mustard seeds, dill seeds, celery seeds, red pepper flakes, allspice, peppercorns, and crumbled bay leaves. Place the mixture on a double-thick square of cheesecloth, gather the corners together, and tie securely with kitchen string to make a pouch. Makes enough to season 5 pounds of shrimp or 12 blue crabs.

Divide the water between 2 large stock pots. Place boil seasoning bag in first pot along with the oil,

onions, celery, lemons, garlic, whole bay leaves, ginger, salt, Creole seasoning, and red potatoes. Bring to a rolling boil and cook for 8–10 minutes, or until potatoes are fork tender. Add corn, cover, and turn heat off. Leave for 8–10 minutes while corn cooks and the ingredients absorb the flavors of the boil.

Remove ingredients carefully, after checking to make sure the corn is cooked and tender, to a clean container; we suggest an insulated cooler to keep temperature hot.

Bring the other pot of clean water to a boil. Add shrimp and cook until the shells separate from meat, about 2 minutes. Turn off heat and transfer shrimp to seasoned water. Let sit for about 10 minutes for shrimp to absorb the flavor of the boil. Remove shrimp from boil, drain, and add to the vegetables. Dump and enjoy. Serve with Cocktail Sauce.

TIPS & SUGGESTIONS

Once the fire under the crawfish or shrimp pot is turned off, the final step is soaking in the boil. The longer the crawfish and company are left in the flavorful boil liquid, the more intense the flavor. So soaking is extremely important and the final step of the boil is the key. Every couple of minutes, grab a crawfish and test the flavor. Once the right amount of spiciness is reached that's when you drain and dump.

COCKTAIL SAUCE

Makes 1 cup

1 cup ketchup

1 tablespoon Worcestershire sauce

1 to 2 teaspoons horseradish

Juice of 1 lemon

1 teaspoon olive oil

Combine all ingredients in a bowl, mix well, and chill in the refrigerator until ready to use.

crawfish Bisque

Whenever I boil seafood, I always boil more than we are going to eat. This is especially true for crawfish. After the eating is done, I invite everyone to stay for what I call the pickin' party. Those who stay are tasked with picking crawfish tail meat for the freezer. And I also have them pop the bodies off the crawfish for stuffing. Stay for the pickin' party and you always get another invitation to enjoy the bisque. **Serves 10 to 12**

STUFFED crawfish Heads

2 pounds crawfish tails, cleaned

1 1/2 cups minced yellow onion

1 cup minced celery

1/2 cup minced green bell pepper

2 tablespoons minced garlic

1/2 cup chopped fresh parsley

3 eggs, beaten

2 cups Italian-seasoned breadcrumbs

2 tablespoons Creole seasoning

Salt, to taste

60 crawfish heads, cleaned, for stuffing

BISQUE

1 1/2 cups vegetable oil

1 1/2 cups all-purpose flour

1 1/2 cups diced yellow onion

1 cup diced celery

1/2 cup diced green bell pepper

2 tablespoons minced garlic

3 tablespoons Creole seasoning

1/4 cup tomato paste

3 quarts seafood stock

1 pound crawfish tails

1 cup chopped green onion

1/2 cup chopped fresh parsley

Salt and pepper, to taste

Hot cooked white rice, optional

STUFFED crawfish Heads

Preheat oven to 350 degrees.

In a food processor, grind tail meat, onion, celery, bell pepper, garlic, and parsley, being careful not to purée into a paste. Place in a bowl, add eggs, and stir to combine. Slowly stir in the breadcrumbs until the stuffing starts to hold together but isn't too dry. Add Creole seasoning and salt; taste to check seasoning.

Stuff heads with equal amounts of breadcrumb mixture. Lay on a baking sheet and bake for 20 minutes, or until lightly browned. Remove and set aside.

BISQUE

In a heavy bottom Dutch oven, heat oil over medium-high heat. Add flour and whisk until you achieve a wet sand consistency. Cook and stir constantly to create a very dark roux, about 12 minutes.

Add onion, celery, bell pepper, garlic, and Creole seasoning and sauté in roux until cooked and starting to wilt, about 3 minutes. Add tomato paste, blending thoroughly. Slowly stir in stock until the mixture begins to take on a loose sauce consistency. Bring to a boil and then reduce to a simmer; add stuffed crawfish heads and simmer for about 30 minutes. Add crawfish tails and simmer for another 10 minutes. Stir occasionally to keep heads from scorching on the bottom.

Remove from heat, stir in green onion and parsley; season with salt and pepper.

To serve, place a small mound of hot rice in the bottom of each individual soup bowl and ladle Bisque over the top.

TIPS & SUGGESTIONS

If you do not have shells, you can take the stuffing and roll it into balls the size of a quarter and follow the recipe.

FRIED LOBSTER WITH CREAMY DILL SAUCE

No, lobsters are not overgrown crawfish. Most of the lobsters we use in New Orleans are from Florida and further up the East Coast. What lobster represents from a culinary standpoint is elegance and tradition. I created this dish to simplify lobster and make it super approachable. Lightly frying adds a texture to the fresh and bright meat that, combined with the cream sauce, is simply lovely. **Serves 4**

Vegetable oil

4 lobster tails, meat removed and cut into bite-size chunks

1 1/2 cups whole milk, divided

1/2 cup all-purpose flour

3 tablespoons Creole seasoning

1 teaspoon garlic salt

1 teaspoon celery seeds

1/2 teaspoon pepper

2 cups fine yellow cornmeal

2 eggs

Heat oil to 350 degrees in deep fryer. Combine the lobster tails and 1 cup milk in a bowl and refrigerate for 20 minutes.

Place flour in small mixing bowl. Add the Creole seasoning, garlic salt, celery seeds, pepper, and cornmeal; mix well. Whisk eggs in separate bowl.

Remove lobster from refrigerator and discard soaking milk.

Dip lobster chunks in the cornmeal mixture, the remaining milk, and then cornmeal mixture again. Batter 5-6 pieces at a time. Gently drop into the hot oil and fry until golden brown, 2-3 minutes. Remove and drain on a paper towel. While frying, prepare the next batch of battered lobster. Serve with Creamy Dill Sauce.

TIPS & SUGGESTIONS

Fry hot and quick. These nuggets only need 2-3 minutes in the oil.

CREAMY DILL SAUCE

Makes 2/3 cup

1/3 cup mayonnaise

1/3 cup sour cream

1 tablespoon minced fresh dill

2 teaspoons grated horseradish

1 teaspoon fresh lemon juice

1/4 teaspoon garlic powder

Kosher salt and pepper, to taste

Fresh dill sprig, to garnish

Combine mayonnaise, sour cream, minced dill, horseradish, lemon juice, garlic powder, salt, and pepper together in a small bowl. Mix well and adjust salt and pepper if needed. Chill in refrigerator, covered, for at least 1 hour. Garnish with dill sprig and serve.

CUBAN CONNECTION

The Belton household has always been colorful—personalities, conversations, and celebrations. All sides of my family are deeply imbedded in New Orleans. The food, the music, and the feeling of family, no matter if blood relatives or relatives by choice, we all belong to New Orleans.

It's really amazing that I found myself much in the same situation as my father. Living with my kids and their grandmother and working together to raise them. Only this time around, my kids got to grow up learning about New Orleans as well as the other part of their family background—Cuba.

New Orleans is strongly connected to Cuban culture, especially through the food and music. New Orleanians enjoyed the quick plane rides to Havana in the 1960s to dance and gamble in the beautiful hotels. And by most accounts, the Cuban architecture isn't too different from that of the French Quarter. Both cultures eat beans and rice. We love seafood, and embrace the coastal style of living. And the music. The Cuban beats have so much soul, just like the soul of New Orleans Jazz music.

LAGNIAPPE

Plantains are closely related to the banana. Plain and simple. The difference is really pretty basic. Skins on a plantain are thicker, and they grow a bit larger, although they ripen the same, green to yellow to black. The main difference is that a plantain is best enjoyed cooked. That is because the starch content is high and the sugar content is lower. The lower sugar means the flavors are much more subtle when fresh, and almost bitter when they are green, but peel, slice, and fry up a plantain and serve in place of a vegetable side with beans, pork roast, or rice and you have an incredible savory delicacy.

Traditional Flan

The French and the Spanish both make flan. With those origins, Creole chefs were making flan here in New Orleans no matter which flag was flying over the Cabildo at Jackson Square. Of course today you can find flan in myriad New Orleans restaurants. I personally love the flan at Lola's on Esplanade Avenue. (It's where I get my paella too, for the record.) **Serves 8**

3/4 cup sugar

1 tablespoon water

4 eggs

1 (14-ounce) can sweet-
ened condensed milk

1 (12-ounce) can
evaporated milk

1 tablespoon vanilla

1 quart boiling water

Preheat oven to 325 degrees.

In a saucepan over medium heat, add sugar and water, stirring continuously with a wooden spoon, until the sugar caramelizes and turns a light brown color. Immediately transfer the syrup to a glass pie dish and tilt in a circular motion until the syrup covers the entire bottom of the dish.

In a mixing bowl, beat the eggs. Add condensed milk and evaporated milk and stir to completely incorporate. Add vanilla and stir. Pour egg mixture in dish over melted sugar.

To create a water bath, pour boiling water in large 3-inch-deep baking pan. Fill half way with boiling water. Place filled pie pan into water bath and place in oven. Bake for about 50 minutes, or until flan is set. Remove from oven and cool. Run a dull knife around the edge of the flan to loosen and invert onto a serving dish. Delicious served warm or chilled.

TIPS & SUGGESTIONS

Stay on top of the cooking time to ensure that the flan cooks through. This can also be made in ramekins for individual portions. Cook in a water bath for 30 minutes until the flan is set. You might want to double the batch. There never seems to be enough for seconds and thirds for all those hungry family members and friends.

Marinated Roast Pork Mojo with Plantains

My boys' Cuban grandmother, Aleida Barerra, made a killer mojo. "Lela" (because the boys couldn't pronounce abuela, *the Spanish word for grandmother) introduced me to this classic wet marinade using ingredients that surprised me. Her roasted pork, marinated overnight, was incredible. This mojo is pretty much her recipe and I'm so happy to pass it along to my kids. With New Orleans' strong Cuban connection, it's nice for Kevin and Jonathan to also share this connection through their Cuban-Louisiana roots.* **Serves 8**

Roast Marinade Mojo

3/4 cup olive oil

1 cup chopped cilantro

1 tablespoon orange zest

3/4 cup freshly squeezed orange juice

1/2 cup freshly squeezed lime juice

1/4 cup roughly chopped mint leaves

10 cloves garlic, rough chopped

1 tablespoon chopped fresh oregano

2 teaspoons cumin

1 teaspoon salt

1 teaspoon freshly cracked pepper

Pork Roast

1 (3 1/2- to 4-pound) pork roast, cleaned, rinsed, and fat cap removed

Mojo

3 tablespoons reserved pan drippings

Reserved marinade

1 tablespoon freshly squeezed lime juice

1/4 cup freshly squeezed orange juice

Salt and pepper, to taste

Fried Plantains

1 quart vegetable oil

3 whole green plantains

1 teaspoon kosher salt

Roast Marinade Mojo

Place all ingredients in a blender and pulse until combined.

Pork Roast

Place pork roast in a large ziplock bag and add marinade. Seal tightly and turn bag several times to coat the roast in the marinade. Place in pan and refrigerate overnight for best results.

Preheat oven to 325 degrees.

Remove roast from marinade and place in baking pan with a rack insert to elevate roast off bottom of pan. Reserve marinade and set aside. Cover pan

loosely with aluminum foil and bake for 2-2^1/$_2$ hours, or until roast reaches internal temperature of 145 degrees. Remove foil and continue to bake an additional 30 minutes.

Remove from oven and place cooked roast on serving dish; reserving pan drippings. Cover with foil and let rest for 15 minutes before serving.

MOJO

In a saucepan over medium-high heat, add pan drippings, marinade, lime juice, orange juice, and salt and pepper. Bring to a boil, reduce to a simmer, and cook for 5 minutes. Taste to adjust seasonings. Serve over pork roast.

FRIED PLANTAINS

In a cast iron skillet, heat oil over high heat until bubbling.

Peel and slice plantains into 1-inch-thick pieces. Fry in hot oil in small batches for 2 minutes on each side until golden brown. Remove from oil and drain on paper towels. Place fried plantains on a brown paper bag, and smash. Return smashed plantains to hot oil in small batches and fry for an additional 3 minutes until crisp. Refresh oil as necessary and always allow oil to come up to temperature between batches. Sprinkle with salt.

TIPS & SUGGESTION

I suggest you marinate the roast for at least 24 hours for best results. My wife, Monica, prepares this in the afternoon for dinner the next night.

Caribbean-Style Paella

*Growing up in Louisiana, eating rice at every meal was one of those little things that connected me to Lela. She had the same experience growing up in Cuba. So it was great that I didn't have to explain how important and ordinary it was to make sure rice was always on the table. The paella dish she taught me how to make was a trade-off for my teaching her how to make jambalaya. I am so grateful for her and her influence in helping me raise my boys as a single father, and keeping the kitchen alive with amazing food and love. **Serves 6 to 8***

---

4 tablespoons olive oil

1 onion, chopped

4 cloves garlic, minced

1 green bell pepper, chopped

1/4 pound andouille sausage, chopped

2 skinless, boneless chicken breasts, chopped

1 1/2 cups Arborio rice, uncooked

5 cups chicken stock, divided

1/2 cup dry white wine

2 teaspoons chopped fresh thyme

2 pinches of saffron threads

1 teaspoon kosher salt

1 teaspoon freshly cracked pepper

2 tomatoes, seeded and chopped

1/2 cup green peas

1 pound (12-count) fresh shrimp, with heads

1/4 cup chopped flat-leaf parsley for garnish

1 lemon, sliced, for garnish

Heat oil in a paella pan over medium heat, about 1 minute. Add onion, garlic, and bell pepper and sauté until onion is translucent, about 3 minutes. Add sausage, chicken, and rice; cook and stir for 3 minutes. Add 3 cups of stock, wine, thyme, and saffron; stir. Add salt and pepper and bring to a boil, about 5 minutes. Reduce heat to a simmer and cook for 12-15 minutes, stirring occasionally.

Check rice, and if it needs more cooking time, add additional stock, about 1 tablespoon at a time, up to the remaining 2 cups; simmer until rice is completely cooked. Add tomatoes and green peas and continue to cook until peas are al dente about 3 minutes. Place shrimp on top of rice and cover to steam, about 2 minutes, or until shrimp turn pink. Remove from heat and cover tightly with aluminum foil. Let sit for about 5 minutes to allow the steam to penetrate the shrimp. Garnish with parsley and lemon slices.

Tips & Suggestion

Put the seafood in at the very end of the cooking time to make sure that it does not overcook.

LOUISIANA YAMS

Do you call them sweet potatoes or do you call them yams? The LSU AgCenter says sweet potatoes began to be marketed as Louisiana yams in 1937 "to distinguish them from the many other sweet potato varieties grown elsewhere at the time." Louisiana sweet potatoes have come to be known as Louisiana yams, and regardless of what you call them, they are just plain delicious!

When the kids were little, I had a routine with the yams. I would bake them on Sunday night and have them ready for the week. I would turn them into mashed yams, yam cakes, and even heat them up for breakfast. A lot of kids don't like them. My kids did and still do.

Momma would make a dish she called candied yams. It looked like sliced orange potato halves painted with shellac. It was glorious to behold and even more so to eat. I think she used a little butter, milk, sugar, and a touch of cinnamon.

I have tried to make them in the oven, I've tried starting them on the stovetop and then moving them to the oven, and I've tried them a thousand other ways. I cannot duplicate her dish. It drives me crazy. It's really the one recipe she made that I've yet to master.

LAGNIAPPE

There is nothing more Southern than a pot of greens cooking on the stove. The flavors of the pungent greens combined with some sort of pickled meat or hambone become Southern table manna. Collard greens are part of the same family as kale, arugula, mustard greens, cabbage, Brussels sprouts, and broccoli. Full of vitamins, particularly vitamin C, calcium, and manganese collards impart nutrition and goodness just like the rays of a sunny, southern day. Greens are simply super healthy. And, don't forget the broth. We Southern chefs often refer to the liquid released from the slow simmer of the greens as "pot liquor."

Creole-Brined Chicken with Roasted Collards and Yams

With the bitterness of the greens and the sweetness of the yams, I've created a certified Southern union of flavors. I also highly recommend brining your chicken to create what always turns out to be a super juicy and tender bird; maybe the best you'll ever taste. **Serves 4**

Creole-Brined Chicken

1 cup kosher salt

1 quart boiling water

1 (2 1/2- to 3 1/2-pound) whole chicken

3 quarts cold water

2 tablespoons butter, room temperature

2 tablespoons freshly cracked pepper

1 tablespoon Creole seasoning

1 cup flat-leaf parsley leaves, free of stems

2 bay leaves

2 teaspoons dried marjoram leaves

1 tablespoon roughly chopped fresh rosemary

1 shallot, peeled and chopped

Roasted Collards and Yams

1 quart chicken stock

3 cups roughly chopped collard greens, stems removed and reserved

2 Gala or Pink Lady apples, unpeeled, cored and diced (reserve cores)

1 red onion, peeled and sliced 1/8 inch thick (reserve peels)

Juice of 1 grapefruit

4 sprigs fresh rosemary

4 sprigs fresh thyme

2 bay leaves

1/2 cup dry sherry

3 yams, peeled and cubed

3 tablespoons grapefruit zest

1 tablespoon Creole seasoning

3 strips cooked bacon, crumbled

Creole-Brined Chicken

Combine salt and water in a 2 quart saucepan. Bring to a boil, and then let cool.

Place the chicken in a large stainless steel bowl or plastic tub that will fit in the refrigerator, and cover with the cold water. Add the salted hot water. Let cool and place in the refrigerator overnight and for at least 10 hours. Make sure the chicken is completely submerged in the brine. Place a weighted bowl on top of the chicken to keep it from floating in the brine, if necessary.

Continued

After brining, remove chicken, rinse, and pat dry. Place chicken in a baking pan on an elevated rack and return to the refrigerator to allow to air dry for at least 3 hours. This will ensure that the skin crisps during the baking process.

Preheat oven to 475 degrees.

Rub the chicken with butter and season inside and out with pepper and Creole seasoning. Stuff the inside of the chicken with parsley, bay leaves, marjoram, rosemary, and shallot. Using kitchen twine, truss the chicken.

Place the chicken on the roasting rack inside a roasting pan and bake for 20 minutes, or until skin begins to brown. Reduce temperature to 350 degrees and continue roasting for 20-25 minutes, or internal temperature reaches 170 degrees.

Remove from oven and place on serving platter. Allow chicken to rest for 15 minutes before serving. Serve with Roasted Collards and Yams on the side.

ROasTeD collarDS anD Yams

Preheat oven to 400 degrees

In a small saucepan, bring stock to a boil; add collard stems, apple cores, onion peel, grapefruit juice, rosemary, thyme, bay leaves, and sherry. Bring to a boil and reduce by half. Reduce heat and simmer for 5 minutes. Remove from heat, strain, and set aside.

Place yams, collard greens, apples, and onion in a large ovenproof casserole dish. Cover with strained stock, sprinkle with zest, Creole seasoning, and crumbled bacon. Bake, covered, for 30 minutes. Uncover and roast an additional 15 minutes.

TIPS & SUGGesTIONS

Brining is really an easy effort. Make room in the fridge and do it. Once you brine, your chicken will always be fine.

sweet potato ravioli

Stuffed ravioli with sweet potato filling truly pops with flavor. With the brown butter sauce on top, the flavors really explode. I think of this as a light, but filling pasta dish. **Serves 6 to 8**

Easy Pasta

3 1/2 cups all-purpose flour, divided

4 eggs

1 teaspoon vegetable oil

1/2 teaspoon salt

Sweet Potato Filling

1 cup ricotta cheese

2 cups mashed cooked sweet potatoes

1/4 cup grated Parmesan cheese

1 egg yolk

1 tablespoon fresh thyme leaves

1 teaspoon ground nutmeg

1 teaspoon ground cinnamon

1/2 teaspoon salt

1 egg

1 teaspoon water

Pecan Brown Butter

1/2 cup unsalted butter

1/2 cup chopped pecans

1 teaspoon chopped fresh thyme

Salt and pepper, to taste

Easy Pasta

On a clean surface, place 3 cups flour in a mound. Make a deep well in the center of the mound and add the eggs, oil, and salt. With a fork, begin mixing the eggs and oil into the flour, incorporating a little at a time. Once fully incorporated you will have a stiff dough. Begin kneading the dough, using a little bit of the remaining flour if it is too sticky, and dampen your hands to make working the dough a bit easier. Dough is ready once it becomes smooth and elastic, about 10 minutes of kneading. An indent should bounce back immediately. Roll into a thick tube, wrap in plastic wrap, and refrigerate for 1 hour.

Sweet Potato Filling

In a food processor, combine ricotta, sweet potatoes, cheese, egg yolk, thyme, nutmeg, cinnamon, and salt until smooth.

In a separate bowl, whisk the egg and beat in water to make an egg wash; set aside.

Remove dough from refrigerator and roll out on a lightly floured surface to 1/4-inch thickness. Cut into 2-inch squares with a knife or a ravioli cutter. Place about 1 teaspoon of the filling in the center of half of the pasta squares. Brush edges with the egg wash and place a pasta square on top of each; press edges together with a fork to seal.

In a large stock pot, bring salted water to a boil. Gently add ravioli and boil until cooked, 6–7 minutes. Remove and drain.

Pecan Brown Butter

In a saucepan on medium heat, melt butter and cook until butter turns golden brown, 2-3 minutes. Add pecans, thyme, salt, and pepper. Remove from heat and serve over ravioli.

Tips & Suggestions

For more of a sweet potato flavor, you can reduce the ricotta and increase the sweet potato by the same ratio.

SWEET POTATO MASH WITH CRUMBLED TOPPING

Sweet? Savory? It's both! This dish came to the family when Monica and Noah joined the clan. The difference from those other sweet potato casseroles is the addition of the banana. Banana gives the dish a more complex flavor and depth. It's not like you can put your finger on it. It just is delicious. Try this for your next holiday celebration. **Serves 6 to 8**

---

5 to 6 sweet potatoes, cleaned	1 cup honey	3/4 cup light brown sugar
4 to 5 bananas, unpeeled	Kosher salt, to taste	1 1/2 cups chopped pecans
1 cup butter, room temperature, divided	3/4 cup all-purpose flour	1/2 cup oatmeal

Preheat oven to 375 degrees.

Prick the sweet potatoes all over with a fork, place in a roasting pan, and roast for 40 minutes. Put the bananas into the pan and continue roasting for 10-15 minutes, until both the bananas and potatoes are very soft. Remove pan from the oven but don't turn the oven off.

When the potatoes are cool enough to handle, scoop out the flesh into a large mixing bowl. Peel the bananas and add them to the bowl with 1/2 cup butter and the honey. Season with salt and beat until combined and fluffy. Spoon into an ovenproof serving dish and smooth the top.

In a separate mixing bowl, use your fingers to rub together the remaining butter, flour, brown sugar, pecans, and oatmeal until mixture is the consistency of coarse crumbs. Sprinkle crumb mixture evenly over the sweet potatoes and return to the oven. Bake for about 20 minutes, or until the crumbs are golden. Serve hot.

TIPS & SUGGESTIONS

If you love bananas, add even more to the recipe. Also, the riper the banana, the better. Overripe bananas are sweeter as they have developed more sugars and are mushier too, which makes combining that much easier.

CROATIA—
THE ADRIATIC INFLUENCE

There are not many restaurants in the world that I would stand in line for. As a matter of fact, the only one I can say for certain that I would wait outside to get a table was the world famous Uglesich's on Baronne Street. It's not there anymore. But my memories of the culinary magic that took place there will never fade.

I've been at Uglesich's in the afternoon when Mr. Anthony and Ms. Gail, the husband and wife duo who ran this hallowed space, received the daily seafood delivery. Nothing frozen. Just fresh, fresh everything. They were such seafood experts that to watch them pick and choose what was acceptable was an educational experience. I really valued seeing them work with seafood.

The same held true for Drago's restaurant in New Orleans. Tommy Cvitanovich, Mr. Drago's son, told me his dad was a stickler for making sure the seafood was super fresh. His signature dish, baked oysters that are charred and grilled to perfection, has become ubiquitous in New Orleans alongside Antoine's Oysters Rockefeller.

Many Croatian families, who long ago settled in Louisiana, are known for their oyster harvesting. It's these families who have kept New Orleans full of bivalves for generations. Oyster boats are nothing like fishing boats. They are long and flat, usually with a tarp over the middle to keep things cool. The motor hums and whines as the harvest net drags

the bottom and is directed over the deck where the expert harvesters dump and sort the haul.

My favorite places to have raw oysters are nestled right on the banks of Lake Pontchartrain. There are numerous old school dining spots that focus on seafood caught right out of the lake.

LAGNIAPPE

Louisiana is situated in the western part of what many refer to as the "Southern grits belt." From Texas to Virginia, grits are commonplace as a breakfast staple served with cheese, bacon, and a side of eggs. In many parts of the South, shrimp and grits are popular.

Grits as a food staple is first referenced in the sixteenth century in Virginia when Native Americans introduced grits to the early settlers. Grits in the Mississippi River valley can trace its food heritage to the Choctaw Indians. The Choctaws, and other tribes, harvested corn throughout the valley. Ashes of the open cooking fires blew into the cooking corn, and the lye in the ash created an effect that allowed the corn to blossom faster, resulting in a quicker cooking time. Thus solidifying corn, and ground corn as grits, into a food staple passed on by the original Louisianans—Native Americans.

creole Baked oysters

This recipe is my take on the traditional New Orleans-style baked oysters. The tang of the Creole mustard with bacon, combined with the traditional seasoning blend of Creole cooks, enhances the salty flavors of the oysters without masking the intention of the dish. ***Serves 4 to 6***

---

3 cups coarse salt

18 fresh oysters, on the half shell

1/2 cup Italian breadcrumbs

2 teaspoons Creole mustard

1/4 cup chopped flat-leaf parsley

1 teaspoon Creole seasoning

1/2 teaspoon pepper

1 cup salted butter, softened

1/2 cup grated Parmesan cheese

4 slices bacon, cooked and crumbled

1 lemon, cut in wedges

Preheat oven to 450 degrees.

Sprinkle the salt evenly in the bottom of a shallow ovenproof dish. Nestle the oysters in their shell, or ceramic baking shells, in the salt.

In a mixing bowl, combine the breadcrumbs, mustard, parsley, Creole seasoning, pepper, butter, and cheese. Top each oyster with about 1 teaspoon of the mixture. Divide bacon evenly among oysters.

Bake for about 10-12 minutes, or until oysters begin to curl and topping browns. Serve with lemon wedges.

TIPS & suggestions

I always remind people to watch the cooking time on the oysters, so as not to overcook. Also, if you can't get oysters in the shell, just use a small ramekin with 3 oysters for a terrific appetizer.

SHRIMP WITH SMOKED GRIT CAKES

My dad always made grits for breakfast. He'd make a pan of grits and pour it into a baking dish to cool. Then he would fry a little fish to go with the grits that he had cut into triangle shaped cakes and sautéed in a little butter. He'd cut from the pan all week. Fish for breakfast was a normal thing for all of us. Usually the fish was courtesy of Uncle Chet; super fresh and lovely. I took inspiration and decided to do it with shrimp. I must say it is a perfect compliment.

Serves 4 to 6

SMOKED GRIT CAKES

3 cups chicken stock

1 cup heavy cream

1/2 cup salted butter

1 teaspoon pepper

1 teaspoon Creole seasoning

1 teaspoon garlic powder

1 teaspoon onion powder

1 cup slow-cook stone-ground grits

1 cup grated cheddar cheese

1 cup grated Monterey jack cheese

1 teaspoon hot sauce

2 cups Italian breadcrumbs

4 eggs, beaten

2 cups all-purpose flour

2 teaspoons Creole seasoning

1 teaspoon pepper

1 teaspoon garlic powder

2 cups vegetable oil

CREOLE SHRIMP SAUTÉ

5 strips thick-cut applewood-smoked bacon, chopped

1/4 cup minced shallots

1/8 cup finely chopped red bell pepper

1/2 cup heavy cream

1 cup creamed corn

1 1/2 teaspoons Creole seasoning

1 tablespoon chopped fresh thyme

1 pound (16/20 size) shrimp, shelled and deveined

Salt and pepper, to taste

2 tablespoons finely chopped fresh parsley

SMOKED GRIT CAKES

In a large saucepan over medium-high heat, bring the stock and cream to a slight boil. Add the butter, pepper, Creole seasoning, garlic powder, and onion powder and continue to heat until boiling. Add grits and whisk constantly for about 2 minutes. Reduce heat to low, cover, and cook for 30 minutes, or until cooked; stirring occasionally.

Once grits are cooked, add a little broth if necessary so the grits don't thicken too much. Stir in cheeses and hot sauce and blend completely.

Butter a glass baking dish and pour in grits. Cover and refrigerate until set, 3-4 hours, or overnight. Remove from refrigerator, cut grits into squares, and place in smoker.

You can make a smoker using a large stock pot with a steamer insert, aluminum foil, and 2 cups pecan wood shavings. Prepare pot by lining the bottom with foil. Place wood shavings on top of foil. Top loosely with another layer of foil and place steamer insert in pot. Place grit cakes evenly in the steamer basket. Place lid firmly on pot and seal tightly with foil. Place pot on stove top and turn heat on high. Let smoke generate for about 10 minutes. Turn off the heat and let the grit cakes rest for 5 minutes.

If you have a strong kitchen hood, turn the fan on high prior to removing lid. Or take the pot outside, remove lid, and allow smoke to escape before bringing back into the kitchen.

Prepare the dredging ingredients by placing breadcrumbs, eggs, and flour in separate bowls. In a small bowl, combine Creole seasoning, pepper, and garlic powder, and divide among the 3 bowls; mix well.

Heat the oil to 350 degrees in a cast iron skillet. Dredge the smoked cakes in the flour, followed by the egg wash, and then the breadcrumbs. Fry in oil for 2 minutes per side until golden brown. Remove and drain on a paper towel.

creole Shrimp Sauté

In a large sauté pan over medium-high heat, cook bacon until crispy. Remove bacon to drain on a paper towel and transfer fat to a separate bowl.

Return pan to heat with 2 tablespoons of bacon fat. Add shallots and sauté until translucent, about 2 minutes. Add bell pepper and sauté until soft, about 2 minutes. Add cream, corn, Creole seasoning, and thyme. Stir thoroughly. Add shrimp and

cook until pink and firm, about 7 minutes. Season with salt and pepper and serve over Smoked Grit Cakes; garnish with reserved bacon and parsley.

TIPS & Suggestions

You do not have to smoke the grits to get a great dish. Also, the grit cakes are a super side to most any dish, steak or roast pork for example. We keep a pan of grits in the fridge for just that reason. Topped with a fried egg, grit cakes make a simple brunch dish too.

Pan-Fried Trout with Anchovy-Jalapeño Gravy

This is my version of Mr. Anthony Uglesich's dish he called Muddy Water. Mr. Anthony is a culinary genius and is one of my most admired New Orleans restaurateurs. He retired after Hurricane Katrina. This dish is one of my favorites. My sauce is a little thicker than the Uglesich version, so I consider it an homage, not a copy. **Serves 4**

Pan-Fried Trout

4 (6-ounce) trout filets

1 tablespoon Creole seasoning

1 egg

1 teaspoon water

1 cup breadcrumbs

$1/2$ cup butter

Anchovy-Jalapeño Gravy

$1/4$ cup vegetable oil

$1/4$ cup flour

4 anchovy filets

6 cloves garlic, sliced

1 jalapeño, seeded and sliced

2 cups chicken stock

Pan-Fried Trout

Rinse and pat the fish filets dry. Sprinkle both sides of the filets with Creole seasoning.

In a shallow bowl, beat together the egg and water. Dip fish in egg wash and then roll in breadcrumbs. Melt butter on medium heat in skillet and cook filets for 3-5 minutes per side depending on thickness of fish. Place on a serving platter when cooked.

Anchovy-Jalapeño Gravy

Heat oil in skillet over medium heat. Stir in the flour and cook roux until it reaches a peanut butter color. Mash anchovies into the roux. Add garlic and jalapeño and stir well. Slowly stir in stock until you achieve desired consistency. Serve over fish.

Tips & Suggestions

Not a fan of anchovies? Add $1/2$ teaspoon soy sauce as a substitute.

GONE FISHIN'

In 1999 I worked for the BBC with an English Chef named Kevin Woodford. When he came to visit New Orleans, I wanted to take him to a traditional seafood restaurant out on Lake Pontchartrain. It wasn't until he started looking at the menu and after the drinks came that he said, "Oh my goodness, do you people fry everything here?" I love that.

And yes, we New Orleanians do fry everything that doesn't fry us first. We're pretty dang good at it, too. But we do know how to cook fresh seafood without frying. It just might not seem that way when you are out and reading the menus all over town. Maybe because of all the nuances of frying at home, and the mess, seafood restaurants really became popular and renowned for their fried platters. My family loves to go out to eat fried seafood.

At home, we gravitate toward the more classical seafood preparations, especially *en papillote* style. I get everybody involved in folding the bags and filling them with the fish, fresh herbs, and vegetables. It's widely known that Antoine's, a landmark restaurant in the French Quarter that opened in 1840, really popularized the en papillote style. It is one of my favorite spots, and I continue to be inspired by not only their cuisine, but by the attention to detail they have consistently shown for more than 150 years. Opening the steaming paper bag is quite a flourish for the delicious find inside.

LAGNIAPPE

There is nothing better than picking the meat off a perfectly boiled Louisiana blue crab. Known as a "swimmer crab" these creatures spend their lives swimming in the sweet salty waters of the Gulf, bayous, and brackish waters of Lake Pontchartrain right here in New Orleans proper. The meat of a cooked blue crab is sweet and light in texture.

You can visually determine the sex of the blue crab, the males have blue tip claws and the females have red tips, like she just got a manicure. The female blue crab will produce a large yellow sponge under their abdomen two to nine months after mating. That sponge averages two million eggs, but can carry up to eight million eggs depending on the size of the crab. It is illegal in Louisiana, and most other states, to possess a female with a sponge.

Soft shell crabs are simply blue crabs that are molting their exoskeleton. This occurs naturally, but there are some crab farmers who induce the molting in controlled settings. That's how many chefs obtain the crabs on a regular basis. The entire crab will remain soft for about two weeks in the wild, making it vulnerable to predators of which humans are tops here in Louisiana. A soft-shell crab can be battered and fried then eaten whole.

TrOUT en Papillote WITH BLUe CraB BUTTer

The presentation and drama of this dish makes it exciting and pretty. The food in a paper pouch brought out by a server and then cut open to reveal a puff of steam—it's culinary theatrics. But the show is not what this is all about. By creating the pouch and steaming all of the ingredients together, you achieve an infusion of flavors that makes this classic "in paper" preparation a true culinary technique. You can't achieve this same flavor profile by steaming in a basket and placing a lid over the pot. You lose the flavors. I find this to be simple and fun to do with really not too much fuss. The results are always spot on. **Serves 4**

1/2 cup plus 2 tablespoons Blue Crab Butter

1 yellow onion, thinly sliced

1 fennel bulb, trimmed and sliced

1/2 cup dry white wine

12 ounces fresh spinach, washed, stems removed

Kosher salt and white pepper, to taste

4 (6-ounce) trout filets

1 tablespoon Creole seasoning

1 tablespoon chopped tarragon

1 tablespoon lemon zest

Vegetable oil

2 cups heirloom grape tomatoes, cut in half, divided

1 lemon, cut in wedges

In a large skillet, melt 2 tablespoons crab butter over medium heat. Sauté onion and fennel and cook until caramelized, about 12 minutes. Add wine and simmer, scraping browned pieces from the bottom of the pan, about 1 minute. Raise heat to high; add spinach and cook, stirring constantly, until spinach is wilted, 2-3 minutes. Season with salt and pepper, remove from heat, and set aside.

Rinse filets and pat dry with paper towels. Season filets on both sides with salt, pepper, Creole seasoning, tarragon, and lemon zest.

Preheat oven to 350 degrees.

Divide sautéed vegetables into 4 servings. Cut 4 (15-inch) squares of unwaxed parchment paper. In the center of each parchment square, place a serving of sautéed vegetables, 1 trout filet, and 1/2 cup grape tomatoes. Fold parchment over the vegetables and filet and seal at the edges with ends joined, making tiny folds and a hard crease, working your way around the paper until the edges are tightly sealed.

Place parchment bags on a baking sheet and bake until bags are fragrant and puffed, about 15 minutes. Remove and transfer to individual serving plates. Serve with lemon wedges on the side.

Parchment bags are available at most grocery stores, making this super easy.

Blue Crab Butter

Makes 1 1/2 cups

2 live blue crabs

1 1/2 cups salted butter, divided

2 teaspoons Creole seasoning

1 teaspoon kosher salt

1/8 teaspoon cayenne pepper

In a medium saucepan, place a steamer insert and bring about 2 inches of water to a rolling boil. Hold live crabs with tongs and rinse thoroughly under cold running water. Place crabs in steamer basket, replace lid tightly, and steam until crabs are bright in color and cooked through, about 10 minutes.

Remove crabs from steamer and let cool. Crush with a meat mallet, breaking up the legs and exposing some of the meat. Place crabs back in saucepan. Add 1 1/4 cups butter and seasonings and heat on low, melting the butter and bringing it to a slow simmer. Stir occasionally while continuing to crush the shells, and cook for about 30 minutes.

Remove from heat and cool for about 15 minutes. Strain the butter through a fine mesh strainer into a small heatproof bowl, making sure to press all of the solids and extracting all of the butter. Once strained, place the bowl over an ice bath to cool and solidify butter. Whisk butter until firm, about 1 minute.

Cube the remaining butter into 1/2-inch pieces. Transfer infused butter to a food processor or blender and add the cubed butter. Process on slow speed until well-blended. Transfer to a small bowl and refrigerate until set, about 2 hours.

Seared Gulf Tuna with Greens and Cilantro, Lime, and Honey Vinaigrette

Certain ingredients, as we all know, have their soul mate. Tuna with citrus is one of those combinations. We are all familiar with canned tuna, à la your momma's famous tuna fish salad. This isn't your momma's tuna fish. This is the rite of passage for those palates who think they don't like tuna. Purchase the tuna steaks the same day you plan on making this dish.
Serves 2 to 4

Vegetable oil, for brushing

2 (6-ounce) tuna steaks

1 tablespoon Creole seasoning

5 ounces mixed salad greens

Salt and freshly cracked pepper, to taste

In a skillet with a griddle surface, lightly brush with oil and place on medium-high heat.

Brush both sides of each tuna steak with oil and sprinkle generously with Creole seasoning. Place steaks on griddle and cook until the tuna releases easily from the hot surface, about 2 minutes. Turn and repeat cook time on other side.

Remove to a plate to rest. Slice on the diagonal with a sharp knife; steaks should be medium rare.

Place greens in a large mixing bowl and toss with enough Cilantro, Lime, and Honey Vinaigrette to coat. Divide and place greens in the center of each individual salad plate and arrange sliced tuna over top. Season with salt and pepper.

TIPS & Suggestions

Hesitant to cook a tuna steak because you are worried about germs? Don't be. Think about it like this. That tuna steak is super fresh and you purchased it from a reputable source the same day you are cooking it. Any bacteria would always be on the outside of the meat or fish in this instance. Once the exterior of the tuna steak touches the heat, any bacteria are eradicated. That's why you can cook filets of beef or fish steaks rare. Ground meats are just that, all ground up, and any potential bacteria could make its way inside, outside, and more.

CILANTRO, LIME, AND HONEY VINAIGRETTE

Makes 1 1/2 cups

1 cup fresh cilantro

1/2 cup extra virgin olive oil

1/4 cup freshly squeezed lime juice

1/4 cup honey

1 jalapeño pepper, seeded and chopped

2 cloves garlic, minced

1/4 cup satsuma orange, blood orange, or freshly squeezed navel orange juice

1/2 teaspoon kosher salt

1/2 teaspoon freshly cracked pepper

1/8 teaspoon minced garlic

2 tablespoons apple cider vinegar

1/2 teaspoon salt

Combine all ingredients in a blender and purée on low until fully blended, about 1 minute. Refrigerate until ready to serve.

WHOLE ROASTED DRUM WITH VEGETABLES EN BROCHETTE

By cooking a fish whole, the flavor from the bones and fats that lie between the skin and flesh intensifies the final dish. It's just another level of extracting the subtle flavors from one of my favorite Gulf fishes. I prefer this cooking method when I can get my hands on a whole fish. Make sure to pick the meat from the cheeks, too. It's my favorite and I consider it a personal reward. **Serves 6**

VEGETABLES EN BROCHETTE

1 cup whole red and yellow cherry tomatoes

2 whole peeled golden beets, cut into cubes and parboiled

1 green bell pepper, cut into chunks

2 cups halved baby red potatoes

1 red bell pepper, cut into chunks

1 cup pearl onions

6 (10-inch) wooden skewers, soaked in water for 10 minutes

1/4 cup sunflower oil

4 cloves garlic, chopped

Juice of 1 lemon

1 tablespoon Creole seasoning

1/2 teaspoon kosher salt

1/2 teaspoon freshly cracked pepper

WHOLE ROASTED DRUM

1 (4- to 5-pound) whole drum, cleaned with head and tail on

1 tablespoon vegetable oil

Salt and pepper, to taste

1 cup parsley, with stems

4 cloves garlic, crushed

1 whole lemon, sliced

1/2 cup dry white wine

VEGETABLES EN BROCHETTE

Thread vegetables on the skewers in the following order: cherry tomato, beet, green bell pepper, potato, red bell pepper, and onion.

In a small bowl, whisk the oil, garlic, lemon juice, Creole seasoning, salt, and pepper together to make a marinade. Place kabobs in a shallow glass dish and cover with marinade. Cover with plastic wrap and refrigerate for 1 hour.

To cook, place the kabobs in a baking pan and bake in the oven with the fish for 40 minutes or until the potatoes are tender.

WHOLE ROASTED DRUM

Preheat oven to 400 degrees.

Place whole fish in a shallow baking pan. Brush with oil and season with salt and pepper, both on the outside and inside the cavity. Stuff cavity with parsley, garlic, and lemon slices. Add wine to pan.

Bake until fish reaches an internal temperature of 145 degrees, 40–45 minutes. While baking, spoon some of the juices back over fish. Fish will be flaky and white when fully cooked.

TIPS & SUGGESTIONS

Make sure to thoroughly coat the whole fish with oil before seasoning. Don't be stingy with the oil. You want that fish to release easily from the pan when serving.

PECANS-
LOUISIANA'S FAVORITE NUT

"Okay. Great! I'll come over and get them," only meant one thing when Mom was talking on the phone. Mom's friends were calling for her to come pick up brown Schwegmann grocery store bags filled to capacity with pecans right off the tree.

I'd watch Nan crack those pecans just right. She was an expert with her silver-hinged nutcracker and her pick. She expertly welded that pick to remove any trace of the bitter membrane. We cracked nuts for days until the brown paper bags that lined the kitchen were empty and what was left were pecan halves bagged and stored for the holidays. Mom used them for pecan pies, sweet potato pies, baked yam casseroles, salads, and on her chocolate cake. She also candied them, and we ate them as snacks.

Foods in season give you a sense of place and enjoyment. Today, we have such convenience that we have access to strawberries in October or watermelon in January. But the best ingredients are the freshest when they are in season. Pecans are the ingredient that first taught me this important culinary concept.

LAGNIAPPE

Good names like Elliot, Jackson, Sumner, and Candy might seem like you are introducing the children of an Uptown New Orleans family. But in actuality, these are the names of the best yielding varieties of pecan trees in Louisiana. These varieties are known as "improved," because these crop yielding trees are products of improvements by grafting onto rootstock to continue to improve taste and yield as well as disease resistance.

The first noted improvements of pecans are widely attributed to a man named Antoine, a first-name-only slave from New Orleans. In 1845 Antoine created a pecan cultivar by grafting pecan branches to a controlled rootstock. This led to a planting of an orchard of 126 pecan trees, thus beginning a long history and relationship between the pecan and Louisiana. Antoine's pecan variety was later named "Centennial" in honor of winning the Best Pecan Exhibited at the Philadelphia Centennial Exposition in 1876.

Peach and Spinach Salad with Roasted Pecans and Goat Cheese

I like a crunch in salad. But a crouton doesn't do it for me. I prefer my bread with salad to be warm slices of French bread. To give this salad a crunch, I discovered that toasted pecans provide a texture and nuttiness that perfectly complements the earthy spinach and the sweet peaches. And of course, the pecans are so very Louisiana. **Serves 4**

---

2 cups whole pecans

9 ounces fresh spinach, about 4 cups

3 tablespoons balsamic vinegar

$1^1/_2$ tablespoons extra virgin olive oil

Kosher salt and freshly cracked pepper, to taste

2 tablespoons salted butter

3 ripe unpeeled peaches, diced

6 ounces fresh goat cheese

Preheat oven to 325 degrees.

Place pecans on a small baking sheet. Place in oven and toast until nuts begin to release oils, about 5 minutes. Remove, cool, and roughly chop. Set aside for garnish.

In a large salad bowl, toss spinach with vinegar and olive oil. Season with salt and pepper. Arrange spinach on 4 individual plates.

In a large sauté pan, melt butter over medium-high heat until bubbling, about 3 minutes. Add peaches and sauté until they begin to brown, about 3 minutes. Remove and drain. Divide peaches among the plates, and finish with a sprinkle of pecans and goat cheese over the top.

TIPS & SUGGESTIONS

Toasting the pecans allows the oils to release, which intensifies the flavor and makes the pecans firmer in texture.

Pecan cheesecake
With caramel Whiskey Sauce

Everyone is looking for that perfect cheesecake. I think what is going to get you to perfection is really all about the perfect topping. I know some experts will argue that texture is what drives their hunt for the perfect cheesecake. Dense or lighter texture? They are all good to me. What counts is the sauce. You can bypass my cheesecake (even though I think it's pretty darn good) but don't bypass this sauce. **Serves 8**

Pecan crust

2 cups whole pecans

3 teaspoons butter, melted

1/2 teaspoon vanilla

3 tablespoons dark brown sugar

1 teaspoon water

Pecan cheesecake

4 (8-ounce) packages cream cheese, room temperature

1 1/2 cups sugar, divided

1/4 cup cornstarch

1 tablespoon vanilla

2 eggs

3/4 cup heavy cream

1 cup pecan pieces

Caramel Whiskey Sauce

1 cup sugar

1/3 cup water

1/4 pound butter

1/2 cup heavy cream

1/3 cup whiskey, of choice

1/4 cup pecan pieces

Pecan crust

Grind pecans in a food processor until fine. Add butter, vanilla, brown sugar, and water and process until mixture is thoroughly blended. Press mixture into the bottom of a 9-inch springform pan. Place pan on several sheets of aluminum foil and secure foil around the sides of the pan.

Pecan cheesecake

Preheat oven to 300 degrees.

In a large bowl, beat 1 package of cream cheese, 1/2 cup sugar, and cornstarch together on low until creamed, about 3 minutes. Scrape down sides of the bowl and blend in the remaining cream cheese, 1 package at a time, scraping down the sides of the bowl after each addition.

Beat in remaining sugar and vanilla on medium speed. Add eggs, 1 at a time, until completely blended into cream cheese. Stir in pecans and gently spoon mixture into crust.

Place filled springform pan in the center of a large shallow pan containing hot water, about 1 inch deep. Bake until the edges are golden brown and the top is light brown, about 2 hours. If cheesecake

is soft at the sides, bake an additional 10 minutes. When done, remove springform pan from the water bath and place pan on wire rack to cool for 2 hours. Once cooled, cover with plastic wrap and refrigerate for at least 6 hours or overnight. Must be completely cold before serving.

When ready to serve, release pan and remove cake. For easy slicing, dip a knife into warm water before cutting each slice.

caramel whiskey sauce

Place sugar and water in a small saucepan over medium heat. Once sugar has dissolved, add butter and cook until golden brown. Remove from heat and whisk in the cream. Return pan to heat and slowly bring back to a boil, reduce heat and simmer for 10 minutes, stirring occasionally. Stir in whiskey and simmer for 5 more minutes until sauce begins to thicken. Remove from heat and add pecans. Serve over cheesecake.

TIPS & suggestions

The sauce stores for up to 1 week in the refrigerator in a covered container. It's great on pancakes, ice cream, waffles, pound cake, pain perdu (French toast), or even the back of your hand!

pecan-crusteD BakeD CHICKen

When most folks make this dish, they crust the chicken with shredded potatoes. I wanted a baked chicken dish that sings with Louisiana inspiration. So I experimented, and came up with this recipe by just adding the chopped pecans along with the breadcrumbs and seasoning to create a topping variation that showcases our beloved nut. (The pecan, not me!) **Serves 4**

---

1 cup toasted whole pecans

$^1/_2$ cup Italian breadcrumbs

2 teaspoons dried basil

$^1/_8$ teaspoon salt

$^1/_8$ teaspoon freshly cracked pepper

4 chicken leg quarters, with skin

$^1/_4$ cup Creole mustard

Olive oil

Preheat oven to 400 degrees.

In a food processor, grind pecans into fine crumbs being careful not to over process into paste. Place pecan crumbs into a large shallow bowl. Add breadcrumbs, basil, salt, and pepper. Mix thoroughly.

Rub each chicken piece with Creole mustard and then coat with breading. Place on a large baking sheet and lightly drizzle with oil. Bake for 18-20 minutes, or until chicken juices run clear.

TIPS & suggestions

Prefer breasts? Follow recipe and adjust the cooking time to 30-35 minutes in the oven at 400 degrees.

LATIN AMERICA MEETS NOLA

Back in 2008, I was invited by the Colegiatura Colombiana in Medellin, Colombia, to be part of a Louisiana delegation of chefs to talk about Creole-style cooking. We also had the honor of serving some of our signature Louisiana dishes during their annual music festival. Imagine that, a music festival serving food. That is so in our wheelhouse. We Louisianans love a good festival, especially one with music and food. We do that so well here.

Even though Medellin is located in the middle of the country, they brought some Colombians from the coastal area to go hand-in-hand with what we do in Louisiana cooking. To see these women cook with the fresh ingredients found in their coastal waters took care of any homesickness I had. The processes and approaches were very familiar. And you know what was more important? They coaxed me into tasting so much food. The spirit of the cuisine and the excitement shared was a mirror reflection of the enthusiasm we have for our cuisine. They were cooking their soul food.

I had arepas at least twice a day. I lost my mind trying to taste all of the different fillings that you can stuff inside an arepa. I think of the arepa as something akin to our po' boy sandwich. And in the same way, the sancocho, is a kindred soup to our gumbo. I loved this food and I really felt a connection and the similarities to my Creole cooking roots. I also was very curious as to how I was going to find these dishes back home.

That's where my wife Monica comes into the picture. It just so happens she is Colombian and has taught me how to make wonderful arepas. I leave the sancocho to her. Both of these dishes are definitely her and Noah's soul food. And now mine, too.

LAGNIAPPE

Masa arepas is packaged precooked cornmeal flour essential to making arepas. The process for making this flour is incredibly labor intensive. It requires the pounding of the whole dried corn kernels to separate the seed germ and outer lining from the remaining part of the corn kernel. Absent the germ and lining, the remaining parts are then cooked and ground and can then be made into arepas. I don't normally advocate skipping steps in the kitchen, but in this case, buy the pre-cooked cornmeal flour. You can find it in most Latin grocery stores and online.

Sancocho

*Sancocho is a Spanish soup with origins in the Canary Islands. And right outside of New Orleans, you'll find the historic Isleños of Louisiana. These Canary Island immigrants settled in St. Bernard Parish, a mere six miles downriver of New Orleans. Sancocho is also prevalent in other Latin American cultures with strong ties to New Orleans such as Honduras, Ecuador, Panama, and the Dominican Republic. Of course the Colombian version is special to my heart as my wife cooks it at home regularly. The backbone of sancocho varies from country to country, but the spirit is the same; slow simmered with seasonal or regional ingredients that offer comfort and sense of place. **Serves 8***

---

1 1/2 pounds oxtails, cut into 2-inch pieces

2 tablespoons olive oil

5 cloves garlic, minced

1 1/2 pounds top round beef, cut into 1 1/2-inch cubes

1/2 cup chopped onion

12 cups chicken stock

1/2 cup of Aliño Sauce

Salt and pepper, to taste

3 ears fresh corn, cut into pieces

2 green plantains, peeled and sliced into 2-inch pieces

1 pound yucca, peeled and cut into big pieces

6 medium potatoes, peeled and halved

1/2 cup chopped fresh cilantro

Hot cooked white rice

Avocado slices, optional

Place the oxtails in a large pot and cover with water. Cook on medium heat for 30 minutes. Remove the oxtails from the pot and rinse them with water.

While the oxtails are cooking, add the oil, garlic, beef, and onion to a 16-quart stock pot over medium heat. Stir and cook until beef is browned on all sides and onions begin to caramelize.

Add chicken stock, Aliño Sauce, salt, and pepper. Bring to a boil then reduce to a simmer. Cover and let simmer for about 1 hour. Skim the fat and add the corn and oxtails; simmer for 1 hour more.

Add the plantains, yucca, and potatoes and continue to cook for 35 minutes. Add more stock if necessary. Stir in the cilantro and serve over white rice. You might be tempted to top with a few avocado slices (it's delicious!).

TIPS & SUGGESTIONS

Oxtail is traditional in the Colombian version of sancocho. Fish, pork, and beef are combinations of other versions and are perfect substitutions.

ALIÑO SAUCE

Makes 1 1/2 cups

1/2 green bell pepper, chopped

1/2 red bell pepper, chopped

1/2 medium onion, chopped

4 scallions, chopped

1/2 teaspoon cumin

3 cloves garlic, crushed

1 cup water

1/2 tablespoon Sazon Goya with Azafran

Place all ingredients into a food processor and process into a thick sauce.

SHRIMP CEVICHE WITH AREPAS

Occasionally when offering ceviche to guests, they've quickly responded, "I don't eat raw fish." And I get that. But this version of ceviche brings a careful approach to the dish ensuring that you aren't actually eating "raw" anything. It's perfectly acceptable to parboil your shrimp or fish for a safe experience and then add the traditional preparation. I love this variation on a traditional preparation as it allows folks living far from the coast to make this healthy and flavorful dish. **Serves 8**

SHRIMP CEVICHE

2 to 3 pounds (36/40 size) shrimp, peeled and deveined

Juice of 6 limes

Juice of 6 lemons

Juice of 2 oranges (preferably sour oranges)

1/3 cup olive oil

1/2 red onion, finely diced

1/2 cup chopped green onion

2 large tomatoes, diced

1 serrano pepper or 1 jalapeño, finely diced

1 bunch cilantro, diced

2 large avocados, diced

2 large cucumbers, peeled and diced

Salt and pepper, to taste

AREPAS

2 cups precooked white cornmeal

1 teaspoon salt

1/2 cup cream cheese, softened

1/2 cup sour cream

2 cups lukewarm milk, divided

1/2 cup vegetable oil, plus extra if needed

SHRIMP CEVICHE

Blanche shrimp in boiling water for about 2 minutes; remove shrimp and place in an ice water bath. Drain the shrimp when they have cooled and cut into 1-inch pieces; place in a large bowl.

Add lime, lemon, and orange juices, oil, red onion, green onion, tomatoes, pepper, and cilantro; marinate in the refrigerator for 4 hours. Add avocados and cucumber and season with salt and pepper before serving.

AREPAS

Place cornmeal and salt in a large bowl. Add cream cheese and sour cream. Stir in 1 cup of milk and mix to thoroughly combine. The dough should be soft and moist, so you will need to add additional milk in small amounts until you get a supple texture. This is not like yeast dough that needs to rise.

Divide dough into golf ball-size balls and pat each down into a patty, about 1/2 inch thick.

Heat a griddle pan and brush very thoroughly with oil. Place arepas, you may need to cook in batches,

on hot griddle and cook first side for 4–5 minutes (do not move the arepas once on the pan). Flip to cook other side for 4–5 minutes. Once cooked on both sides, transfer to a plate to cool.

TIPS & SUGGESTIONS

Parboiling is the key to ensure that the shrimp are not raw, but are also not overcooked. Marinating the shrimp up to 12 hours will intensify the flavor.

Guava Turnover

Guava is a tropical fruit that flourishes in Mexico, Central, and South America. It's easily found in your Latin grocery store either canned, or in a log in paste form. I'll eat a thin slice of guava paste with Swiss cheese, and my wife Monica loves it spread on top of cream cheese. As a filling for a turnover, it's outstanding and is a delicious signature flavor of the Americas. **Serves 4**

1 tablespoon sugar

1 (1-pound) package puff pastry

4 to 6 ounces guava paste, thinly sliced

1 egg, beaten

2 teaspoons water, divided

1/4 cup powdered sugar

1/2 teaspoon lemon juice

Preheat oven to 400 degrees.

Sprinkle the sugar on a clean, dry work surface to prevent the dough from sticking. Roll out each sheet of puff pastry and cut into 8-inch squares.

Place the squares on your work surface like a diamond, and add guava paste a little off the center to the left or the right. Beat egg with 1 teaspoon of water and brush the edges of the square with beaten egg. Fold the upper half of the square over the filling to make a neat triangle and crimp the edges with a fork. Repeat for other pastries and place them on a parchment paper-lined baking sheet.

Bake for 20 minutes, or until golden brown.

While pastries are baking, mix the powdered sugar with remaining water and lemon juice; stir to dissolve any lumps. Drizzle glaze over cooled turnovers.

TIPS & Suggestions

For a different take on the recipe to satisfy a savory and sweet craving, add a thin slice of cream cheese or queso blanco inside the pastry before baking.

BUTTER UP

Grandma Emily asked me, "Kevin, do you think I should start eating margarine?" She had to have been about seventy-five years old at the time.

I said, "Grandma, all these years you cooked with butter. You use lard. You save every drop of bacon drippings in that CDM coffee can. If God wanted to you to eat margarine, he would have put it in a cow."

It was the answer she was looking for. Grandma Emily lived well into her eighties.

I think one big mistake people make with their cooking is they think more is better. It only takes a little bit of butter to add a whole lot of flavor. Too much butter makes a dish or sauce too greasy.

From my French cooking roots, I learned to finish vegetables with butter at the end of the cooking time to add shine and creaminess. In a meunière sauce, butter goes in at the end to cream the sauce and finish the flavor. I use butter in savory dishes to add a little extra complexity.

When it comes to desserts, you have to follow the recipe exactly not only when it comes to butter but to the rest of the measured ingredients as well. As we all know with pastry baking, it's more like chemistry and there's not much room to change the ratios when you are combining butter with sugar, flour, and eggs. It even matters when you change the order of the ingredients.

When I teach folks how to make bread pudding, I always want them to take a taste of it before the butter. Then I have them taste it after I add the butter. Often they can't believe the taste difference. Even an untrained palate tastes the change after the addition of butter.

There is nothing better than butter. And a little bit goes a long way.

LAGNIAPPE

Onions are members of the allium family, and that includes green onions, scallions, and shallots. Shallots have a much milder flavor than onions and have almost a garlic essence. The milder flavor translates very well in more elegant and restrained dishes, especially in Creole cooking. Shallots can be confused with green onions, so be careful what you buy at the store. Shallots will not deliver the same flavor as a green onion. Green onions have a much sharper flavor, and we use them uncooked to finish or garnish dishes such as gumbos and étouffées to add visual as well as flavor brightness. Shallots, on the other hand, develop flavor when cooked.

HOMEMADE BACON POPCORN TOPPED WITH CLARIFIED BUTTER

"Go big or go home" was my mantra during my sports days. I find that this mantra works well when I need inspiration for a new dish. I needed an oil to pop some corn, and I decided bacon grease would work. The bacon flavor really popped through and layered flavors exceptionally well. When we finished the popcorn with seasoning, the triple flavor profile made this the best popcorn I've ever tasted. **Serves 4**

POPCORN

1/4 cup bacon grease or rendered bacon fat

2/3 cup popcorn kernels

1 1/2 teaspoons kosher salt, or salt of choice

CLARIFIED BUTTER

1 pound unsalted butter

CREOLE-SPICED POPCORN SEASONING

1/4 cup clarified butter

1 1/2 tablespoons sweet paprika

1 tablespoon garlic powder

1 tablespoon thyme

1 teaspoon pepper

1 teaspoon dried oregano

1/2 teaspoon cayenne pepper, or to taste

2 teaspoons salt

POPCORN

In a heavy-bottom pan, heat grease on medium-high heat with 3 kernels of corn until the kernels pop, about 4 minutes. Remove popped kernels.

Pour in popcorn and stir with a wooden spoon to coat kernels. Place lid on pot and continue to heat until you hear the kernels begin to pop. Turn off heat. With lid tightly secured, shake pot to ensure that all kernels pop. Continue to agitate until the popping slows, 1-2 minutes.

Remove from heat and immediately transfer to a large serving bowl. Sprinkle with salt and Clarified Butter, or top with Creole-Spiced Popcorn Seasoning.

CLARIFIED BUTTER

In a large saucepan on medium-high heat, melt butter and allow to boil. Continue boiling until it forms a foamy white surface then eventually clears and stops bubbling. Remove from heat and strain through a cheesecloth or coffee filter into a glass jar. Clarified butter can be stored in an airtight container for 3-4 weeks, or in the refrigerator for several months.

CREOLE-SPICED POPCORN SEASONING

Heat clarified butter over medium heat until bubbling. Add spices and stir. Continue to heat for 1 minute. Remove from heat and pour over hot popped corn.

TIPS & SUGGESTIONS

Make sure you do the three-kernel test to ensure
your pan heats up. Popcorn pops better and
faster, and by better, I mean most all the kernels
will pop if you start with a hot pot. Also, use a
good quality popcorn rather than cheap stuff.

SPINACH LASAGNA WITH BLONDE BÉCHAMEL

This lasagna, made without the traditional red sauce, is a sublime take on the usual. An unexpected smoothness comes through with the béchamel taking the place of the red sauce. You could call this a three-cheese lasagna because in addition to the ricotta, I add mozzarella and Gruyère to the béchamel. **Serves 6 to 8**

SPINACH FILLING

4 tablespoons butter

1 shallot, minced

2 tablespoons minced garlic

2 pounds spinach leaves, chopped

Salt and pepper, to taste

2 pounds ricotta cheese, divided

2 eggs

1/2 cup grated Parmesan cheese

1 teaspoon freshly grated nutmeg

BLONDE BÉCHAMEL

1/4 cup butter

1/4 cup flour

4 cups whole milk

1 cup grated mozzarella, divided

1 cup cubed Gruyère, divided

2 tablespoons Creole seasoning

1 1/2 to 2 pounds no-boil lasagna noodles (enough for 8 to 10 layers)

SPINACH FILLING

In a saucepan, melt butter. Add shallot and sauté for 2 minutes. Add garlic, stir, and slowly add spinach, allowing it to wilt. Season with salt and pepper. Place spinach in a mesh strainer and press out water using a rubber spatula.

Place 1 pound of ricotta, eggs, Parmesan, and nutmeg in a food processor and blend for 1 minute until smooth. Place mixture into a large mixing bowl. Place spinach into food processor and pulse 10-12 times. Add spinach to bowl along with remaining ricotta. Fold gently to combine.

BLONDE BÉCHAMEL

In a large saucepan over medium heat, melt butter then add flour and stir for 1 minute until golden blonde in color. Slowly add milk, stirring constantly. When mixture comes to a boil, remove from heat and add 3/4 cup of each cheese and seasoning, stirring until smooth.

ASSEMBLING THE LASAGNA

Preheat oven to 400 degrees.

Spread a small amount of béchamel to cover the bottom of a 9- x 13-inch pan. Add a layer of noodles. Top with a thin layer of spinach mixture followed

by a little of the béchamel. Continue layering pasta, spinach, and béchamel until you lay down the top layer of pasta. Spread remaining spinach mixture evenly on top. Sprinkle with remaining cheeses and drizzle with sauce; smooth top using a spatula.

Cover tightly with aluminum foil and bake for 20 minutes. Remove foil and continue baking until bubbly and lightly browned, about 20 minutes.

Remove from oven and let rest at room temperature for 5 -10 minutes. Slice and serve.

TIPS & SUGGESTIONS

The more layers you have with a thin filling between them will produce a final dish that has more pasta per slice and is better balanced. So keep the many layers, it's what makes the dish.

BAKED CHICKEN WITH HERBED BUTTER

It's one thing to season a chicken for baking, that's kitchen basics 101. But by stepping up to this approach, your baked chicken dish will taste so much better. That's why I like to get my seasonings into an oil. It's when the oil heats that the seasonings release flavors. It's worth the extra step to create the herb butter. You'll immediately realize how effective this is from the first bite. **Serves 4**

---

4 boneless, skinless chicken breasts

$1/2$ cup roughly chopped fresh parsley

4 garlic cloves, minced

$1/2$ cup Herbed Butter

Preheat oven to 375 degrees.

Slice chicken breasts lengthwise, but not all the way through to create a pocket. Fill each breast equally with fresh parsley and garlic. Place chicken breasts in a glass baking dish. Evenly divide butter and spread over the top of the chicken breasts.

Bake until done, about 15-20 minutes. Turn chicken breasts several times during cooking to baste in butter and evenly cook.

TIPS & SUGGESTIONS

A whole chicken would also be great for this recipe. Stuff the cavity of the chicken with the parsley and garlic. Lift the skin and pat the Herbed Butter under the skin of chicken by working up from the legs to the breast and other areas. Use a sharp paring knife to get under the skin, but be careful not to cut away the skin entirely. Bake at 375 degrees for 1 hour, or until an internal temperature of 165 degrees. About halfway through the cooking time, baste the entire chicken with Herbed Butter to allow the skin to crisp.

HERBED BUTTER

Makes 1/2 cup

1/2 cup unsalted butter, softened

1 tablespoon chopped fresh basil

1 tablespoon chopped fresh thyme

1 tablespoon chopped fresh sage

1 tablespoon chopped fresh parsley

1 tablespoon chopped fresh tarragon

1 tablespoon chopped fresh oregano

1 tablespoon chopped fresh rosemary

1 teaspoon coarse salt

1 teaspoon freshly cracked pepper

In a small mixing bowl, combine all ingredients thoroughly. Spoon mixture onto a sheet of wax paper in the shape of a log and roll into a thick tube. Twist ends to seal and place in refrigerator. Chill for 1 hour, or until firm.

VIBRANT VIETNAMESE

Growing up, Dad and I would drive all over New Orleans East to fish in some of his secret spots off of Chef Highway. That was a big part of my childhood. In 1981, I bought my first home in New Orleans East and that's where I raised my two oldest sons. I was always in the car exploring the area, and eating and shopping in all of the interesting spots. It was around this time that I discovered the Vietnamese community and the great cultural establishments that include restaurants, markets, and bakeries.

One of my great New Orleans East memories is turning off Chef Highway to make a U-turn to come back to the grocery store. Crossing the bridge, I was totally amazed with what I saw—backyard gardens as far as I could see. I got out of the car to check it out and it was such an incredible sight. I thought, "Wow! No grass to cut!" Seriously though, most all of the residents living in that neighborhood were part of the Vietnamese community.

Gardens, food, culture, and family; all values that fit so easily with Louisiana.

LAGNIAPPE

When shopping for shrimp, cooked or raw, you might notice these numbers on the package; "16/20" or "U15" for example. That simply means the number of shrimp you will get in a pound. Shrimp come to the fish monger, that's the name for the fish and crustacean expert, graded by size. This enables cooks to purchase the shrimp in a size best suited for the dish being prepared. In New Orleans, the most popular spots for barbecue shrimp use U15s, also known as colossal. Those are the big guys. The heads are left on because that's where the flavor is.

vietnamese chicken wings

I love chicken wings. The classic original invented in Buffalo, New York, introduced many people to spicy and sweet flavor combinations. My wing recipe is classical in cooking. With the addition of the spicy Vietnamese sauce, I've created a surprising taste dimension for my version of wings. **Serves 4**

Vegetable oil

10 chicken wings, cut in half at joint

1 teaspoon salt

1 teaspoon Creole seasoning

1 teaspoon garlic powder

¹/₄ cup corn starch

2 tablespoons olive oil

3 cloves garlic, minced

1 pinch plus 1 tablespoon sugar

1 tablespoon fish sauce

¹/₂ teaspoon red pepper flakes

Preheat oil to 365 degrees in a deep fryer.

In a large mixing bowl, add wings, salt, Creole seasoning, and garlic powder. Toss to coat. Dust wings in cornstarch and fry for 8-10 minutes until crispy.

In a saucepan, heat olive oil and add garlic with a pinch of sugar. Cook garlic until crispy; remove and place on paper towel to drain, leaving oil in pan. Add fish sauce and remaining sugar. When sauce starts to boil, add red pepper flakes, stir, and then add the wings. When sauce starts to get sticky, return cooked garlic to pan and stir well. Turn off heat and serve wings on a plate.

TIPS & SUGGESTIONS

Don't be put off by the fish sauce. If it is a new ingredient in your pantry, take solace in knowing that once cooked it takes on a whole new flavor profile. And a little bit goes a long way.

Vietnamese spring Rolls with Peanut Dipping sauce

These fresh, hand rolled hallmarks of Vietnamese cuisine really speak to the clean, simple, and pure cooking that Vietnamese chefs and home cooks are known for. It's what gets me into the car and out to the Vietnamese community in New Orleans East on a regular basis. **Serves 4**

---

1 teaspoon kosher salt

1 tablespoon Creole seasoning

12 (16/20 size) extra jumbo shrimp

8 ounces rice noodles

24 whole fresh mint leaves, stems removed

2 cups romaine lettuce

1 cup julienned carrots

1 cup finely chopped red cabbage

1 cup bean sprouts

1/2 cup roughly chopped cilantro

8 (8 1/2-inch) round rice paper wrappers

In a 2-quart saucepan, bring 4 cups of water to a rolling boil. Add salt, Creole seasoning, and shrimp and boil for 1-2 minutes, until shrimp turn pink. Remove pan from heat (do not drain water) and remove shrimp, placing them in an ice bath to cool for 5 minutes. Return pan to heat and bring cooking water to a boil.

Add rice noodles to water and boil until cooked and tender, about 5 minutes. Drain and place noodles in an ice bath to cool, for about 10 minutes. Drain and refrigerate noodles until chilled, about 30 minutes. Remove shells from cooled shrimp and cut lengthwise in half.

Line up ingredients beginning with mint, shrimp, lettuce, noodles, carrots, cabbage, sprouts, and cilantro.

Fill a large shallow baking pan with water. Submerge rice papers, 1 sheet at a time, until moist and pliable, about 15 seconds. Remove from water and shake off excess. Lay on a dish towel and fill with ingredients in the order listed, using 4 mint leaves, 3 slices shrimp, 1 ounce noodles, 1/4 cup lettuce, 1 tablespoon each of carrots, cabbage, and sprouts, and a sprinkle of cilantro.

Roll and seal the roll onto itself. Line a baking dish with moist paper towels to keep rolls pliable and to keep them from sticking to any surface.

Serve chilled with Peanut Dipping Sauce. If the rolls start to dry out, lightly moisten with warm water.

TIPS & Suggestions

I use cool water to get the rice paper wrappers started. The directions usually say warm water,

Continued

but, I'm telling you, ignore that and listen to Chef Kev. The hot water reconstitutes the paper too quickly for novice hands and it becomes excessively sticky during the filling and rolling process. When you remove the wrappers from the water, place on a clean cotton dish towel while you fill and roll. The towel will absorb excess water and keep the paper from being sticky. Keep wet paper towels handy. When layering them in your glass baking dish, lay the wet paper towel between layers. This will keep the rolls fresh in the refrigerator and allow you to make a couple of dozen at a time. This is an amazing snack and great for those watching their figure.

Peanut Dipping Sauce

Makes 1 cup

1/2 cup hoisin sauce

1 teaspoon soy sauce

1 teaspoon Sriracha sauce, optional

1 clove garlic, minced

1/4 cup smooth fresh peanut butter

1 tablespoon rice wine vinegar

2 tablespoons filtered water

1 tablespoon chopped roasted peanuts

In a mixing bowl combine hoisin, soy sauce, Sriracha, garlic, peanut butter, and vinegar. Add water to reach desired consistency. Garnish with peanuts.

vietnamese won ton soup with shrimp and pork won tons

Chefs speak a lot about their mise en place. "Everything in its place" is the literal translation and comes from the beginning days of the culinary arts. With that in mind, I know this recipe looks like a lot of ingredients and such, but once the prep is done, your mise en place, you won't believe how easy it is to create this dish. New Orleans doesn't have many chilly or downright cold days, but when we do, people flock to the nearby pho restaurant to enjoy this fantastic soup. I do. **Serves 6**

WON TON FILLING

1/2 pound boneless pork shoulder, chopped coarse

1/2 pound shrimp, peeled and deveined, chopped into small pieces

1 teaspoon cornstarch

2 teaspoons Creole seasoning

2 cloves garlic, minced

1/2 teaspoon kosher salt

1/2 teaspoon pepper

2 stalks scallions, whites finely chopped

1 teaspoon sesame oil

24 won ton wrappers

PHO GA (CHICKEN BROTH)

2 large yellow onions, peeled

1 (4-inch long) piece fresh ginger, unpeeled

8 pounds chicken backs

10 quarts water

1 1/2 teaspoons kosher salt

3 tablespoons fish sauce

1 teaspoon sugar

2 tablespoons coriander seeds, toasted

4 whole cloves

2 cups roughly chopped cilantro

WON TON SOUP

4 whole baby bok choy, cut lengthwise

1 cup sliced mushrooms, oyster or shiitake

4 stalks scallions, cut in 4-inch pieces

WON TON FILLING

Combine pork, shrimp, cornstarch, Creole seasoning, garlic, salt, pepper, scallions, and sesame oil together in a medium bowl and mix thoroughly. Fill the center of each won ton with 1 teaspoon of filling. Using a pastry brush, wet the edges of the won tons and fold to form a rosette, twist to seal. Cover with a wet dish towel to prevent drying and sticking.

Continued

To cook the won tons, fill a large stock pot with water and bring to a rolling boil. Gently introduce the won tons to the water using a wire skimmer. Let them cook until they float to the top, about 5 minutes. Then cook for 2 more minutes, remove with skimmer, and place on a plate to drain. Cook in batches of 8 to prevent overcrowding and sticking together.

PHO GA (CHICKEN BROTH)

Preheat oven broiler.

Place onions and ginger on broiler rack and roast under broiler until softened and slightly sweetened, about 15 minutes. Check constantly and turn to prevent over scorching. Remove from broiler and place on gas flame (if possible) and char over flame, turning for an even char, about 2 minutes. Remove and cool. Run onions under cool water to remove blackened pieces, and then cut into quarters. Scrub charred spots from ginger. Crush ginger with the end of a knife. Set aside.

Rinse chicken, and using a meat cleaver, crush completely to break open bones.

Bring 2 large stock pots, each filled with 5 quarts of water, to a rolling boil. Add chicken to the first pot and boil for about 3 minutes to release initial impurities. Remove from boiling water and transfer to a strainer set in a clean sink. Rinse with cold running water. Place chicken in second pot with clean boiling water. Return to a boil and then reduce heat to low. Simmer for 30 minutes.

Remove chicken, discard, and strain impurities from liquid to leave a clean, clear broth. (Make sure to maintain the simmer only, don't let it boil, or broth will turn cloudy and will not be the clear broth indicative of pho.) Add onions, ginger, salt, fish sauce, sugar, coriander, cloves, and cilantro. Simmer for $1 1/2$ hours to infuse flavors. Strain the broth. You should end up with about 4 quarts of broth.

WON TON SOUP

When ready to serve, heat broth and add bok choy, mushrooms, and scallions. Divide broth, bok choy, mushrooms, and scallions evenly into 6 individual serving bowls. Add won tons and season with fish sauce or soy sauce.

TIPS & SUGGESTIONS

If you don't have time or need kitchen therapy, you can substitute the from-scratch pho broth with chicken stock. And if you prefer the more traditional small Vietnamese won tons, reduce the filling amount to $1/2$ teaspoon and make double the amount.

Vietnamese Egg Rolls With Dipping Sauce

The filling in this egg roll is more elegant than most egg rolls. I recreated the stuffing that you find in those very special and complicated stuffed chicken wings known in Vietnamese cuisine. I just bypassed the chicken leg prep and used the ingredients as an egg roll filling. **Serves 6**

Vegetable oil

1 pound ground pork

1 yellow onion, finely chopped

1 clove garlic, finely chopped

1/4 teaspoon garlic powder

2 tablespoons minced lemon grass

Salt and pepper, to taste

4 mushrooms (rehydrated cloud or wood mushrooms), chopped

1/2 cup chopped peanuts

4 ounces clear glass noodles, rehydrated and chopped into small pieces

12 won ton wrappers

Preheat oil to 365 degrees in a deep fryer.

In a large mixing bowl combine pork with onion, garlic, garlic powder, lemon grass, salt and pepper, mushrooms, peanuts, and noodles; mix thoroughly.

Working with 1 wrapper at a time, place the wrapper with one corner of the diamond closest to you, brushing edges with water. Place 1 tablespoon of filling in the center of the wrapper and roll the corner closest to you over the filling. Fold in the sides and continue rolling to close. Press to seal. Fry egg rolls, a couple at a time, for about 5 minutes until golden and crispy.

Serve hot with Dipping Sauce.

TIPS & SUGGESTIONS

You can fill the rolls in advance and keep in the refrigerator overnight. Cook them right before serving. They are better fresh from the fryer.

DIPPING SaUCE

Makes 1 1/2 cups

1/3 cup freshly squeezed lime juice

3 tablespoons sugar

6 tablespoons fish sauce

1/2 cup warm water

3 Thai chiles, thinly sliced

2 cloves garlic, minced

1/4 carrot, julienned

1 scallion, thinly sliced thin

1 tablespoon white vinegar

In a small bowl, combine lime juice, sugar, fish sauce, and warm water; whisk to dissolve sugar. Add remaining ingredients and stir. Cover and refrigerate to chill.

TAILGATING DISHES THAT SCORE

Dad and I would walk over to Tulane Stadium, just a stone's throw from the house, and hang out with his buddies in the parking lot before the Saint's games. That was in the 1960s before the Superdome was built and before I knew what tailgating meant. One time I remember eating a hamburger and hot dog from the grill set up in the parking lot. There were people everywhere shaking hands and getting ready for the game. I was thrilled with the food and the excitement.

In high school I played defensive tackle. I really enjoyed being part of a team. And looking back, there are a lot of similarities between a football team and a kitchen team. Those early days and lessons learned really shaped who I am as a culinarian. Filming our television series is a team effort, too. I think that's why I enjoy it so much.

I loved playing sports, but I hated missing out on the tailgate parties. When push came to shove, the party won out over playing a game. Yes, I chose food over sports, and there hasn't been a day I regretted it. Tailgating is one of the most glorious ways to combine a love of sports with my other love, food. So now I always get the best of both worlds.

LAGNIAPPE

Worcestershire is made from a fermented liquid of anchovy, vinegar, molasses, onions, corn syrup, salt, garlic, tamarind, cloves, chili powder, and other spices. It is a condiment that adds depth and dimension to sauces without adding unnecessary salt. And if you have a barbecue sauce that is too sweet, you can temper that sweetness by adding a bit of Worcestershire sauce, drop by drop, until you achieve the flavor profile you prefer. Several well-known spice makers in Louisiana make special blends using their own secret recipes. My favorite is from Cajun Power Sauce in Abbeville, Louisiana. Worcestershire sauce from scratch is not daunting. You make it and let it set for about 2 weeks. The great thing about making it from scratch is you can leave out the anchovy, if you prefer.

VeGGie CHIPS WITH ReD Bean HUMMUS

Hummus is hip. And the base is always puréed chickpeas, also known as garbanzo beans. So this is my homage, but I've traded the chickpeas for our famous New Orleans red beans. Of course, as with all hummus, homemade is always better than packaged. This version is easy and delicious. **Serves 8**

VeGGie CHIPS

2 beets, peeled and thinly sliced using a mandolin

2 sweet potatoes, peeled and thinly sliced using a mandolin

1/4 cup vegetable oil or coconut oil

1 tablespoon sea salt

ReD Bean HUMMUS

2 cups cooked or canned red beans, rinsed and drained

1/4 cup tahini or peanut butter

1/4 cup olive oil, plus extra to drizzle

2 cloves garlic

1 cup chicken or vegetable stock

Salt and pepper, to taste

Juice of 1 lemon

1 tablespoon ground cumin or paprika

Chopped fresh parsley

VeGGie CHIPS

Preheat oven to 300 degrees.

Place beet and sweet potato slices in a large stainless mixing bowl and toss with oil and salt to thoroughly coat.

Line a baking sheet with parchment paper and place seasoned vegetable slices on sheet in a single layer. Bake until crispy, about 20 minutes. Watch closely after about 12 minutes to make sure that chips are baking evenly. Remove and cool. Store in an airtight container.

ReD Bean HUMMUS

Place red beans, tahini, 1/4 cup olive oil, and garlic in a food processor, or place in a bowl and use a stick blender, and blend to combine. Add stock, a little bit at a time, to obtain a smoother consistency.

Season with salt and pepper and stir in lemon juice. Serve, drizzled with olive oil and sprinkled with cumin and parsley.

TIPS & SUGGeSTIONS

Follow the recipe but substitute white beans, black beans, or any kind of beans, for that matter. Tahini is ground sesame seeds with a flavor profile similar to peanut butter. No tahini in the pantry, just add peanut butter. It will do the trick.

skewered steak, chicken, and shrimp

Tailgate parties evoke a sense of camaraderie among fans from high school and college sports all the way to professional football. Gathering for a tailgate is a rally cry for fans excited about the upcoming event; a modern-day battle of sorts. It's fitting that food plays an important role at tailgates. When I think tailgate party, I think skewered meat on the grill. Skewering and marinating your own kabobs means you can make ahead, pack up, and easily transport to the parking lot or park. We did a field-to-surf-to-turf skewer to cover all the bases in this recipe. **Serves 4**

Marinade

1/4 cup soy sauce

1 cup vegetable oil

1/4 cup Worcestershire sauce

2 tablespoons Creole Seasoning

1/2 cup lemon juice

3 cloves garlic, minced

1/4 cup Creole mustard

2 teaspoons fresh cracked pepper

Kabobs

1 1/2 pounds top sirloin steak, cut in 2-inch cubes

1 1/2 pounds boneless, skinless chicken breasts, cut in 2-inch cubes

24 shrimp, peeled and deveined tails intact

1 red onion, cut in chunks

8 cloves garlic, peeled

1 yellow bell pepper, cut in chunks

8 whole baby portobello mushrooms

8 wooden skewers, soaked in water for about 10 minutes

Marinade

Combine ingredients in a small bowl; set aside.

Kabobs

Alternating ingredients, thread the beef, chicken, shrimp, and vegetables on skewers. Place in a deep pan and pour marinade over each kabob, coating thoroughly. Marinate in the refrigerator for 4 hours or overnight.

Preheat oven to 350 degrees.

Remove kabobs from refrigerator, remove from marinade, and rest at room temperature for 10 minutes. Place kabobs on a baking sheet and put in oven to roast until cooked, about 20 minutes. Turn once during cooking.

You can easily grill these skewers for 8-10 minutes, turning to ensure even cooking.

TIPS & SUGGESTIONS

Soak your wooden skewers to ensure they don't char or flame during cooking.

MIRLITON

Dad carried the classic postman's mail bag—oversized brown leather and filled with mail bundled in rubber bands that he had sorted and organized by hand in the morning before starting his route. Back then, his days started at six in the morning and he might not get home until after six in the evening. Dad ran his route six days a week. I think it's really neat that his route was very close to our house. Everyone knew Dad. He was like a rock star for all the residents between Napoleon Avenue and Louisiana Avenue and from Freret Street to Claiborne Avenue.

Sometimes on Saturday, if Mom needed to find Dad before we headed out to buy groceries, we'd drive over to his route and start asking the neighbors if they had seen him. He ran that mail route for more than 20 years. We usually found him within minutes as the neighbors gladly pointed out whether he had "just been there" or "I just passed him 'round the corner."

It seemed that even though Dad might be at the end of his route, his mailbag never seemed to empty. That's because the residents always gifted Dad with little gestures of appreciation; mirlitons (chayote) were always part of his haul. I don't ever remember Mom buying mirlitons at the store. Apparently Dad could count on a full supply from walking his postal route.

Mirlitons are never in short supply in New Orleans. Once a mirliton vine is established, it will produce with wild abandon. Dad would pass by, drop the mail, and in would go a few mirlitons. Dad loved them. And because of that, Mom cultivated many tricks and recipes that really showcase this special fruit from the vine. Dad made sure to keep bringing them home, so we had mirlitons often. It's funny how so many people have never tried a mirliton, but down here in New Orleans, it's as common place as a 100-degree day in the summer.

LAGNIAPPE

Creole mustard looks totally different from basic yellow mustard. It gets its super tangy flavor from the higher concentration of mustard seeds. You can actually see them floating in the rich, dark golden mustard. It's the spicy brown mustard seeds instead of the more mellow yellow seeds that make this unique condiment. French and German influences give us this special Creole blend much akin to the traditional coarse German mustards and spicy French mustards that these cultures are well-known for.

MIRLITON BREAD

This is a New Orleans version of a classic quick bread. Quick breads are breads that do not use a leavening agent, and Americans love these sweet and savory loaves. The most popular being banana and zucchini breads. My Grandma Emily made fantastic banana bread. We'd eat it, toasted with butter, for breakfast, as a snack with jam, or topped with ice cream. The same with mirliton bread. I love it because it's a recipe so specific to NOLA. **Serves 8**

1/2 cup butter

1 1/4 cups sugar

2 eggs

2 cups cooked and puréed mirliton

2 1/2 cups all-purpose flour

1 teaspoon ground cinnamon

1/2 teaspoon baking powder

1 teaspoon baking soda

2 teaspoons vanilla

1 cup chopped pecans

Preheat oven to 325 degrees. Prepare a 5 x 9-inch loaf pan by buttering and lightly dusting with flour.

In a large mixing bowl, cream together the butter and sugar. Add eggs and mix. Add mirliton purée and continue to mix.

In a separate bowl, sift together the flour, cinnamon, baking powder, and baking soda. Slowly add dry ingredients to the mirliton mixture to incorporate. Add vanilla and pecans. Mix thoroughly.

Bake for 1 1/4 hours for small loaves, or 1 1/2 hours for a large loaf. The loaves are done when a toothpick inserted in the center comes out clean.

TIPS & SUGGESTIONS

Make muffins instead of a loaf in a lined muffin tin and bake for 35 minutes at 350 degrees.

MIRLITON GAZPACHO WITH FRIED OYSTER GARNISH

Gazpacho reminds me of summer in New Orleans, and when the Creole tomatoes become ripe, I always make a batch. The addition of the mirlitons adds a crunch, and they absorb the seasoning, transporting it to your palate. The oyster garnish on top is my New Orleans indulgence.

Serves 8

GAZPACHO

4 large ripe Creole tomatoes (approximately 2 1/2 to 3 pounds), cored and medium diced

2 pounds English cucumbers, peeled, seeded, and medium diced

1 3/4 cups medium diced green bell pepper

1 3/4 cups medium diced yellow bell pepper

1 3/4 cups medium diced red bell pepper

2 1/2 cups medium diced Vidalia onions

1 1/2 poached mirlitons, seeded and medium diced

1 (46-ounce) bottle vegetable juice (like V8)

1 tablespoon minced garlic

1 cup extra virgin olive oil

1/2 cup red wine vinegar

2 tablespoons Creole seasoning

1 teaspoon hot sauce

1/2 cup fresh basil, chopped

Salt and pepper, to taste

FRIED OYSTERS

3 dozen oysters, in brine

1 1/2 cups whole milk

Vegetable oil

2 1/2 cups fine yellow cornmeal

2 cups all-purpose flour

2 tablespoons Creole seasoning

1 teaspoon kosher salt

GAZPACHO

Chill all the vegetables and vegetable juice. Combine all ingredients in a large plastic or non-reactive container. Remove 1/5 of the mixture and purée in blender. Add back to soup and mix to combine. Chill overnight to allow flavors to combine. Serve in chilled bowls garnished with a fried oyster, or serve a few oysters on the side.

FRIED OYSTERS

Drain oysters from brine and transfer to milk. Heat oil to 375 degrees in deep fryer.

Combine the cornmeal, flour, Creole seasoning, and salt in a mixing bowl. Coat the oysters, one at a time, by removing them from the milk and allowing the milk to drip off enough that the oysters are still damp, but not overly wet. Roll each oyster in

the cornmeal mixture to thoroughly coat, patting the coating in where necessary.

Place 6-8 oysters in the oil, being careful not to overfill, and fry until the sides curl, about 1-1^1/$_2$ minutes, and the oysters turn golden. Remove and place on a paper towel to drain.

TIPS & SUGGESTIONS

I often serve this as an appetizer. It's easy to pass around in a little shooter glass. You can still top it with the fried oyster. Go further, shuck some oysters, and use the gazpacho to make an oyster shooter.

BBQ Pork on Brioche with Spicy Mirliton Slaw

Momma used to make a lot of pork dishes. She always saved leftovers and shaved the meat for sandwiches the next day; her version of a BBQ sandwich. Her homemade coleslaw served on the side, like a salad, was the cool touch to the spicy sandwich and sauce. **Serves 10 to 12**

BBQ RUB

1/4 cup brown sugar

1 tablespoon chili powder

1 1/2 teaspoons pepper

1 teaspoon onion powder

1 teaspoon garlic powder

1/2 teaspoon ground cinnamon

2 teaspoons kosher salt

1 teaspoon cumin seeds

1 teaspoon fennel seeds

1/2 teaspoon cayenne pepper

BBQ Pork

1 (8-pound) pork roast

3 large carrots, peeled and chopped in 2-inch chunks

2 drops liquid smoke

2 to 3 cups pork or beef stock

BBQ Sauce

1/2 cup reserved cooking liquid from pork roast

1 1/2 cups packed brown sugar

1 tablespoon finely chopped white onion

6 cloves garlic, minced

1 1/4 cups ketchup

2 tablespoons honey

1/4 to 1/2 cup apple cider vinegar

2 tablespoons Creole mustard

1 tablespoon Worcestershire sauce

Spicy Mirliton Slaw

2 mirlitons, pits and skins removed, julienned

1/2 cup shredded red cabbage

1 1/2 teaspoons salt

2 tablespoons red wine vinegar

1 teaspoon sugar

1/8 teaspoon cayenne pepper

1 teaspoon vegetable oil

1 red bell pepper, julienned

1 jalapeño, seeds removed, chopped

3 tablespoons chopped fresh parsley leaves

Salt and pepper, to taste

10 to 12 brioche buns

BBQ RUB

Combine all ingredients and mix thoroughly.

BBQ Pork

Prepare roast by rinsing and patting dry. Cut into 3 pieces and season thoroughly with BBQ Rub.

Place in pressure cooker. Add liquid smoke and broth. Cook for 45 minutes following manufacturer's directions. When roast is done, remove it from the cooker and place on a platter. Shred the roast using 2 forks. If you prefer, you can reserve 1/2 cup of the drippings from the cooker and combine with shredded meat for additional moistness.

BBQ Sauce

Combine all ingredients in a medium bowl, making sure brown sugar is thoroughly dissolved. Chill for 2 hours, or let set overnight for best flavor. The sauce can be either drizzled over the top of the meat or stirred into the meat according to your preference.

Spicy Mirliton Slaw

Place mirlitons and cabbage in a strainer. Sprinkle with salt and toss. Allow to drain for about 30 minutes to let ingredients shed some water. (This allows for the slaw to remain crisp.)

In a small bowl, combine vinegar, sugar, cayenne, and oil. Whisk thoroughly.

In a medium bowl, combine the mirlitons, cabbage, peppers, and parsley. Pour dressing over slaw and mix thoroughly. Season with salt and pepper. Serve chilled.

To assemble, open buns and place desired amount of meat on the bottom halves. Add extra sauce if you would like, and top with mirliton slaw. Place the top halves of the buns on the sandwiches and enjoy.

Tips & Suggestions

It's best to make this slaw a day ahead to allow for the flavors to develop.

BEANS

I have my bean rules. I'm steadfast. To soak or not to soak, that is the question. The answer is, it depends. I learned to cook beans the way my mom cooked them. Red beans? Soak them, always. Butter beans? Nope. I do sauté them along with seasoning and then add stock and allow them to cook. And, we all know, you cook beans for a long time.

I'm always fascinated that beans start out rock hard and then turn into such a delicious dish. As a kid, I'd always put a bean or two in my mouth. Hard and with no flavor is how I always thought of uncooked beans. But as I became more and more involved with cooking, I became enthralled with the outcome after beans are cooked. With the right seasonings and time to cook down, the result is simply unparalleled. It's when beans are allowed to develop a flavor personality and become creamy and dreamy when I get super-charged with this simple dish. Beans in general don't need any fuss. I always tell people who have trouble making beans to hold back on doing too much with seasoning. Over seasoning just masks the true essence of any bean.

New Orleans-style red beans are a great example of a dish where natural flavor and texture combined with the right spices come together as a true soul food dish and really define the flavor of a culture.

LAGNIAPPE

Bison is lower in fat and the taste is rich, absent a gamey flavor, and is just as tender as high-end cuts of beef. Because bison are raised in open, wild spaces unlike the commercial beef industry, they are consequently grass fed and are maintained without being packed in tight spaces and are not normally given hormones. Depending on the cut, bison has half the calories of beef and a fourth of the fat.

CUBAN-STYLE BLACK BEANS AND RICE

Lela, the boys' grandma, taught me how to make authentic Cuban-style black beans. Her base was onion, garlic, bay leaves, and olive oil. The finish was cilantro. No trinity here, just pure clean flavors. It's such a great memory for me to know that I learned from the real deal and I can pass this along to Kevin and Jonathan for their family traditions. **Serves 6 to 8**

---

3 tablespoons olive oil, divided

$1/2$ cup finely chopped white onion

2 cloves garlic, sliced

2 tablespoons garlic powder

2 tablespoons whole leaves fresh cilantro

1 bay leaf

1 pound black beans, soaked overnight, rinsed and drained

6 cups chicken stock

$1/2$ cup chopped scallions

2 limes, cut in wedges

Hot cooked white rice

In a heavy-bottom saucepan over medium heat, add 2 tablespoons oil. Sauté onion and garlic until onions cook down, about 10 minutes.

Add garlic powder, cilantro, and bay leaf and sauté for 1 minute. Add beans and sauté for 30 seconds. Add stock and bring to a boil then reduce to a simmer. Cook for 45 minutes, or until beans are tender and liquid has reduced to almost nothing. Drizzle with remaining olive oil. Remove from heat and garnish with scallions and lime wedges.

TIPS & SUGGESTIONS

The drizzle of a bit of olive oil over the beans before serving makes this dish. That's how Lela did it.

RED BEAN CHILI WITH JALAPEÑO-CHEDDAR WAFFLE BOWLS

A red bean chili is simply a classic hearty dish. I wanted to revisit this classic and use the red beans we are known for here in New Orleans. Making the waffle bowls means that you can eat everything on the plate! I did fall in love with Hormel canned chili in college. God forbid I told my mother. I don't think I'd had anything out of a can until I left home. I remember one of my roommates would cut up hot dogs and stir them into the Hormel can. Then he'd use the bun as a scoop. Wow. Chili reminds me of college. **Serves 6 to 8**

RED BEAN CHILI

2 tablespoons olive oil

1 pound ground bison or beef

1 1/2 cups chopped onions

2 tablespoons Creole seasoning

1 tablespoon minced garlic

1 cup beef stock

2 cups diced tomatoes

1 cup strong coffee

1 tablespoon tomato paste

1/4 cup brown sugar

1 tablespoon chili powder

1 tablespoon cocoa powder

1 jalapeño, seeded and diced

1 1/2 tablespoons ground cumin

1 teaspoon coriander

2 (15-ounce) cans kidney beans, rinsed and drained

JALAPEÑO-CHEDDAR WAFFLE BOWLS

1 1/2 cups all-purpose flour

2 teaspoons vegetable oil

1 cup cornmeal

1 cup finely grated cheddar cheese

2 teaspoons baking powder

1 tablespoon salt

1 teaspoon pepper

2 eggs, beaten

2 cups whole milk

2 jalapeños, seeded and diced

RED BEAN CHILI

In a Dutch oven or large pot on medium heat, add the oil. When hot, add the meat and sauté, breaking up into crumbles until browned; remove to a bowl and set aside.

Add onions and Creole seasoning and sauté for 1 minute. Add garlic, stock, tomatoes, coffee, and tomato paste; stir well. Add brown sugar, chili powder, cocoa powder, jalapeño, cumin, coriander, and beans. Stir well and return meat to the pot. Reduce heat to low and simmer, partly covered for 1 hour. Taste and adjust seasoning. Continue to simmer on low, stirring often. The longer the chili cooks the richer and more flavorful it will become.

JalapeÑo Cheddar Waffle Bowls

Heat waffle iron according to manufacturer's directions.

Combine the flour, oil, cornmeal, cheese, baking powder, salt, and pepper in a mixing bowl. Stir until mixture is well-combined. Add the eggs, milk, and jalapeños; thoroughly combine. Scoop batter into bowl-shaped waffle iron and cook according to manufacturer's directions. Flat waffles will work fine, just scoop chili on top.

Tips & Suggestions

The second day is always better than the first day when it comes to chili. And it freezes great. You can portion it out and send it off with your family in school or work lunches.

WHITE BEANS AND SHRIMP

This is a total grandma dish. Here's why. All of my friends would say, "I had white beans and shrimp at Grandma's last night." That was the thing. I don't know anybody's mom who made it, including mine. I guess grandmas knew that you cook those white beans, plus enough for a little extra, because they really do compliment the shrimp. The next day you could extend the beans a little more by adding the shrimp, which was always a staple at the house. **Serves 8**

---

3 tablespoons vegetable oil

1 large smoked ham bone

1 1/2 cups finely chopped yellow onion

1 cup finely chopped green bell pepper

1 cup finely chopped celery

3 cloves garlic, minced

1 teaspoon chopped fresh thyme

2 bay leaves, crumbled

1 tablespoon Creole seasoning

8 cups chicken stock

1 pound white beans, soaked overnight, rinsed and drained

1 teaspoon salt

1 teaspoon freshly cracked pepper

1/4 teaspoon cayenne pepper

2 pounds small shrimp, peeled and deveined, with tails

1 tablespoon chopped fresh Italian parsley

Hot cooked rice

1/4 cup sliced green onions

Hot sauce

In a large Dutch oven over medium heat, add the oil. When hot, add the ham bone and sauté for 2 minutes; push to the side. Add onions and sauté for 5 minutes, or until translucent. Add bell pepper and sauté for 2 minutes. Add celery and sauté another 2 minutes. Add garlic and cook until fragrance is released, about 1 minute. Add thyme and bay leaves and sauté for 1 minute. Add Creole seasoning and stir thoroughly, sautéing for 1 minute. Add stock and bring to a boil then reduce to a simmer. Add beans, salt, pepper, and cayenne and cook, uncovered, until beans are tender, about 1 hour. Add shrimp and parsley and cook until shrimp turn pink, about 4 minutes. Remove from heat and serve over rice, garnished with green onions and hot sauce.

TIPS & SUGGESTIONS

Add a little cooked ground meat to the beans or even a paneed pork chop served over the top. Very Creole and delicious.

AUNT DOROTHY'S ARSENAL

Aunt Dorothy, mom's older sister, was born in East Chicago, Indiana. Less than a year old, my great aunt and uncle put her on a train headed back to Canton, Mississippi, alone. Can you imagine? Family history says they phoned Great-Grandma Sarah and Great-Granddad Will and gave them a head's up for a surprise package arriving at the Canton station.

That surprise package, an 11-month-old unescorted baby, was left on a train bound for New Orleans that just passed through Canton. It so happened that Grandma Sarah's neighbor, Ms. Lockette, happened to be on the train coming back from Chicago and noticed the baby with a note pinned to her clothes with a delivery address. When Ms. Lockette realized that the address was across the street from her Canton home, she took charge of Aunt Dorothy with the help of the train conductor.

When the Canton family found out that the Chicago-based brother was due another baby a few years later, they wasted no time and drove up to Chicago. There for the birth of my mother, they whisked her immediately back to Canton. And that's how Nan became the most wonderful mother to the Thomas girls, my mother and Aunt Dorothy. Nan just stepped up on behalf of her brother. She was single at the time and it seemed as though this was meant to be. Nan never wavered on the fact that my mother, Sarah, and Aunt Dorothy were her children. That was never up for discussion. That's the way it was.

These women, all of them, were huge influences on me. The way they conducted themselves under just about any circumstance was with grace and style. Both my mother and Aunt Dorothy cultivated big careers in the 1960s and 70s when women were entering the work force in a meaningful way. And for black women in the South, it wasn't a cakewalk. I embrace the many great qualities of these three powerhouses. They passed on to me the real meaning of what it takes to be a family.

LAGNIAPPE

A great meal isn't just about the food. It's the total experience. Setting a proper table is as important a part of dining as the recipes themselves. Remembering where utensils are placed is as simple as remembering that you use knives, forks, and spoons from the outside in. That means that as each course is served, the outermost utensils of the setting are there to compliment the dish in front of you. It's fun to know how to set a table and pass that along to younger generations. Believe it or not, it can be a game changer out in the world when business is done around the dining table.

Banana Pudding with Sweet Coffee Glaze

Banana pudding was one of those desserts you didn't ordinarily find in a restaurant. But the Beltons always had it at home. It's a true New Orleans comfort food, kept in the fridge in a large bowl. At the time, Mom didn't consider it fancy enough to serve to company. But boy has that changed. **Serves 8 to 10**

Banana Pudding

2 cups crushed vanilla wafers, divided

3 ripe bananas, sliced in 1/4-inch slices, divided

1 3/4 cups sugar, divided

1/4 cup all-purpose flour

2 cups whole milk, divided

3 egg yolks

2 teaspoons butter

2 teaspoons vanilla

3 egg whites

Sweet Coffee Glaze

1 cup strong coffee, regular or decaf

1 teaspoon vanilla

2/3 cup sugar

Banana Pudding

Preheat oven to 350 degrees.

Evenly spread 1 cup of crushed wafers in the bottom of a 9-inch round baking dish, and layer half of the banana slices over the top.

In a medium saucepan combine 1 1/2 cups sugar with flour. Mix thoroughly and add 1 cup of milk. Beat yolks and whisk into mixture. Add remaining milk and butter. Place on low heat and cook, stirring constantly, until thickened, about 10 minutes. Stir in vanilla and remove from heat.

Pour 1/3 of the pudding over bananas while still hot. Sprinkle remaining crushed wafers over pudding and layer with remaining banana slices. Top with remaining pudding mixture.

In a large glass mixing bowl beat eggs whites until foamy. Add remaining sugar and continue to beat until stiff peaks form. Spread on top of pudding layers, completely covering the pudding. Bake for 15 minutes, or until meringue starts to turn golden brown. Remove, cool, and chill before serving. Once chilled, you can either serve from the baking dish or you can spoon into individual dishes for a fancier presentation. Drizzle with Sweet Coffee Glaze.

Sweet Coffee Glaze

In a medium saucepan over medium heat, combine coffee, vanilla, and sugar; whisk until sugar completely dissolves. Continue to cook until mixture is gently bubbling. Reduce heat and simmer until sauce thickens and reduces by half. Remove from heat and cool.

TIPS & SUGGESTIONS

Coffee and banana combined are one of those
soulmate ingredients making the glaze such
a perfect compliment. You can substitute the
vanilla wafers for graham crackers or chocolate graham crackers.

OKRA

Okra is one of those vegetables that you either love or hate. I am thoroughly convinced that people who say they do not like okra have never had it cooked right.

One of the simplest preparations for okra is to cook it with a little bit of oil and diced onion. You just sauté with some Creole seasoning and a little salt and pepper. You will notice as it cooks, a stringy texture appears from the pods. Just keep sautéing that okra until the slime disappears. Add diced tomato and serve the okra as a side vegetable. This simplest of preparations provides a maximum taste. If you like squash, zucchini, eggplant, and such, you should be an okra fan.

LAGNIAPPE

Louisiana is one of six states in the U.S. that grows ninety-nine percent of all rice produced annually. Worldwide there are more than one hundred varieties of rice. In Louisiana, the focus is on production of long, medium, and short-grain varieties. With such an important crop for Louisiana in terms of export and yield, LSU leads the way in research and working with the industry to ensure the yearly harvest is successful. Varieties such as Catahoula, Cheniere and Cocodrie, all recognizable names in Louisiana, round out some of the most successfully planted rice varieties in fields across the state. It's also cool to know that rice is grown in flooded fields. Once the harvest is over, those same rice fields turn into crawfish incubators.

In terms of cooking classic New Orleans dishes, the focus is on long-grain varieties of rice that have less starch. Once cooked, long-grain rice is dryer and separates easily, making it perfect for dishes that have a lot of sauce like étouffée, red beans, and gumbo.

Fried Okra with Pecan Breading

I often hear, "I don't like okra. But I love fried okra." Well okay then. I love it, fried, boiled, smothered, you name it. This recipe really lets the okra shine with the light approach to the breading. You won't think of fried okra the same way ever again. **Serves 4**

---

1 pound whole okra

1 cup pecan pieces

1 1/2 cups all-purpose flour

1 teaspoon salt

1 tablespoon Creole seasoning

1/2 teaspoon cayenne pepper

2 cups peanut or vegetable oil

Rinse okra and drain well. Place okra in refrigerator to chill, about 20 minutes.

Preheat oven to 300 degrees.

Place pecans on a baking sheet in a single layer and roast for 7 minutes, until oils begin to release. Remove and let cool. Process in a food chopper to achieve a coarse chop. Be careful not to over process. You want a consistency that is rough, not a dusting flour consistency.

In a mixing bowl, combine flour and pecan pieces with salt, Creole seasoning, and cayenne.

Heat oil to 350 degrees in a cast iron skillet or deep fryer.

Using the heel of your hand, gently smash okra and roll in flour mixture. Press in pecan pieces to make sure they stick during the frying process.

Fry coated okra in small batches for 5-7 minutes, until golden brown. Turn the okra once to ensure even cooking. Remove and drain on paper towels. Season with salt or Creole seasoning, to taste. Serve hot.

TIPS & Suggestions

You can cut the okra into 1/2-inch pieces if you prefer. Results are the same, simply delicious.

CRABMEAT-STUFFED OKRA

I'd never had this dish before until I created it. I've eaten a lot of crab cakes and I've eaten a lot of okra. I figured why not put them together as I do in my seafood gumbo? This dish gives you a crab cake stuffed inside an okra. What more could you want? **Serves 8**

STUFFED OKRA

1 egg, beaten

1 cup Italian breadcrumbs

3/4 cup dry white wine

1 tablespoon Creole seasoning

2 cloves garlic, minced

1 tablespoon finely chopped Italian parsley

1 teaspoon kosher salt

1/8 teaspoon cayenne pepper

2 teaspoons freshly squeezed lemon juice

1 1/2 cups claw crabmeat

16 extra-large okra pods, rinsed

8 strips bacon, cut in half

2 cups vegetable oil

WASH AND COATING

2 eggs

1/4 cup whole milk

1 teaspoon hot sauce

2 teaspoons kosher salt, divided

2 cups extra fine cornmeal

1/2 teaspoon cayenne pepper

STUFFED OKRA

In a medium bowl, combine the egg, breadcrumbs, wine, Creole seasoning, garlic, parsley, salt, and cayenne. Mix thoroughly. Add lemon juice and stir. Gently fold in crabmeat, being careful not to break up crab.

Slice each okra pod lengthwise to form a pocket, being careful not to cut all the way through. Fill each pod with 2 tablespoons of crab mixture. Wrap each okra pod with a strip of bacon and secure with a toothpick.

Heat oil to 350 degrees in a deep fryer.

WASH AND COATING

In a long, deep mixing bowl, beat together the eggs, milk, hot sauce, and 1 teaspoon salt until thoroughly combined.

In a separate long, deep mixing bowl, mix together the cornmeal, remaining salt, and cayenne.

Working in small batches, dip each stuffed okra pod into the egg wash and then gently roll in cornmeal mixture until completely coated.

Gently fry okra in hot oil until cooked and golden brown, about 7 minutes. Remove from oil and let drain on paper towels. Make sure you remove the toothpicks before serving.

TIPS & SUGGESTIONS

We fried these, however, if you prefer baking to frying, they come out great that way as well. Heat the oven to 350 degrees and bake for 30-35 minutes. Remove and serve warm with a chilled remoulade.

CREOLE-SMOTHERED OKRA AND SHRIMP OVER RICE

Traditionally Creole families often served okra and tomatoes as a side dish. The okra and tomatoes were smothered and seasoned and went with all main ingredients: fish, meat, or pork. Somewhere along the way, my Grandma Emily started to add shrimp to the okra and tomatoes, and wow. When served over rice, it is amazing. **Serves 6 to 8**

---

2 teaspoons vegetable oil

1 cup chopped onion

$1/2$ cup chopped green bell pepper

$1/2$ cup chopped celery

2 cloves garlic, chopped

$1/2$ cup sliced button mushrooms

1 teaspoon salt

1 teaspoon pepper

2 teaspoons Creole seasoning

1 pound okra, rinsed and sliced

2 large tomatoes, diced

$1/2$ cup chicken stock

$1 1/2$ pounds (16/20 size) shrimp, peeled and deveined

Hot cooked white rice

In a large Dutch oven or large skillet, heat oil on medium-high heat. Sauté onion until translucent, about 5 minutes. Add bell pepper and celery and continue to sauté until soft, about 3 minutes. Add garlic and cook 1 minute. Add mushrooms and cook for 2 minutes. Add seasonings and sauté for 1 minute.

Add okra and stir. Add tomatoes and stir. Add stock and bring to a boil then reduce to a simmer. Cover and cook for 10 minutes. Stir in shrimp. Cook for 5-7 minutes until shrimp turns pink. Taste and adjust seasoning if necessary. Serve over hot rice.

TIPS & SUGGESTIONS

Not a fan of shrimp? Leave them out. Or, substitute crawfish or chicken, just adjust the seasoning.

PLAQUEMINE PARISH CITRUS

Lemon juice is my secret culinary weapon. Besides the fact that lemons are my favorite fruit, I believe that adding citrus to many of my dishes elevates the flavor. My wife Monica uses fabric printed with lemons to sew in pockets in my chef coats to hold my microphone rig for filming and presentations. If that doesn't tell ya how much I love lemons then let's talk about how I use them.

You know I love soup. And when I make it, I add lemon juice. A quick squeeze and suddenly you can taste the richness and flavor complexities that might otherwise be missed. I never add salt at the table. I always add lemon. And for that matter, lemon squeezed over black or pinto beans really add a zip and zing that makes a heavy bean dish seem light and bright.

Lemons, as well as, limes, oranges, and satsumas are widely known to provide a level of acidity that can tenderize meat and replace wine in a pan sauce or eliminate vinegar in a dressing. As much as I use lemons, it wasn't until my culinary cohort Rhonda Findley and Monica convinced me to try lemon in mashed potatoes that I knew how good that could be. Now lemon mashed potatoes are my favorite mashed potato dish.

Lemons ripen in South Louisiana in November and hang around until about March. Just across the river from New Orleans in Plaquemine Parish, is where the majority of the citrus groves are found. You'll find farm stands galore running through what we call the Westbank. For those unfamiliar, the Westbank is right across the Mississippi River from New Orleans. And the Westbank is actually east of New Orleans, but that is a complicated story best for another time.

My cousins in Canton, Mississippi, all had lemon trees. My Aunt Lena, Nan's sister, made lemonade that would knock your socks off using lemons harvested practically from her back porch. We would always bring lemons back to Mom, and she'd make lemon pound cake and lemon ice box pie. In our family, when life handed you lemons, you can bet we made something really good to eat!

LAGNIAPPE

South Louisiana is flush with satsuma trees. This citrus fruit looks similar to a tangerine and peels perfectly into segments that are easy to eat and have a bright orange flavor with less acidity than a regular orange. The first satsuma trees planted in and around New Orleans, particularly in Plaquemine Parish, are relatives of the first imported satsumas brought from Japan in the late 1800s and planted in the Florida panhandle. Satsumas thrive here just like they were native plants of South Louisiana.

CITRUS-ROASTED CHICKEN WITH LEMON MASHED POTATOES

Most folks might think the star of this dish is the chicken. As much as I love chicken, I have to admit that the Lemon Mashed Potatoes are what makes this dish stunning. **Serves 6**

CHICKEN

1 cup orange juice

2 tablespoons soy sauce

2 tablespoons honey

2 teaspoons minced garlic

2 teaspoons minced fresh ginger

1 teaspoon lime zest

1/4 teaspoon cayenne pepper

12 chicken thighs

1 tablespoon vegetable oil

1/2 teaspoon kosher salt

1 whole lemon, sliced in 1/4-inch-thick slices

1 whole lime, sliced in 1/4-inch-thick slices

LEMON MASHED POTATOES

6 large Yukon gold potatoes

8 tablespoons butter

2 cups heavy whipping cream

2 cups whole milk

1 teaspoon kosher salt

Zest of 2 lemons

1 teaspoon lemon juice

1 teaspoon freshly cracked pepper

1 to 2 tablespoons olive oil

CHICKEN

In a large ziplock bag, combine the juice, soy sauce, honey, garlic, ginger, zest, and cayenne; mix well. Add chicken, seal bag, and toss to coat. Marinate in the refrigerator for 2 hours. Turn bag a few times to make sure all pieces are equally marinated.

Preheat oven to 425 degrees.

Arrange citrus slices in the bottom of a glass or ceramic baking dish, and place chicken on top. You can add marinade to baking dish and baste during oven roasting if you would like to.

Bake for 60 minutes, or until chicken reaches internal temperature of 160 degrees. Remove from oven and let rest for 10 minutes.

LEMON MASHED POTATOES

Rinse potatoes, peel, and cut into 1-inch cubes. Add potatoes to a large pot of water, bring to a boil, and cook until softened, about 12 minutes. Drain in a colander and return to hot pot.

Add butter and mash with a manual masher to incorporate and melt butter. Add cream and milk, 1/4 cup at a time, until desired consistency is achieved. Add salt, zest, juice, pepper, and oil. Mix to combine. Adjust seasoning and serve warm with chicken on top of the potatoes.

TIPS & SUGGESTIONS

Use satsumas or limes in the same way as
the lemons to change things up. The orange
mashed potatoes have a sturdiness that goes
great with grilled meat. The lime-flavored
potatoes finish a piece of baked fish perfectly.

salt-crusted pompano with satsuma butter sauce

I love pompano because the flavor is mild and the meat is flaky with almost an ocean sweetness. If I see pompano on the menu, that's always what I order. I wanted to try an interesting cooking technique and challenge with this recipe. What the salt dome accomplishes is that it allows the fish to steam in its own juices in a much more intense way than covering the baking fish with foil or a lid. The salt crust leaves no space for the moisture from the fish to escape, and the results are a very moist fish with the flavors from the stuffing thoroughly infused throughout. **Serves 4**

salt-crusted pompano

2 whole pompanos, cleaned with heads and tails intact

1 tablespoon kosher salt

1 tablespoon pepper

1/2 cup cilantro leaves

1/8 cup chopped red bell pepper

1/8 cup thinly sliced red onion

1/2 cup halved cherry tomatoes

1 teaspoon kosher salt

2 teaspoons Creole seasoning

6 egg whites

4 cups kosher salt

satsuma butter sauce

4 satsumas

4 tablespoons unsalted butter

3 tablespoons apple cider vinegar

1 shallot, minced

2 teaspoons Creole mustard

2 stalks green onion, thinly sliced

3 tablespoons vegetable oil

1 teaspoon kosher salt

1 teaspoon freshly cracked pepper

1/2 teaspoon hot sauce

salt-crusted pompano

Preheat oven to 450 degrees.

Rinse the fish inside and out and pat dry. Place on a baking sheet and season with 1 tablespoon salt and pepper.

In a small mixing bowl, combine cilantro, bell pepper, onion, tomatoes, 1 teaspoon salt, and Creole seasoning. Mix thoroughly. Divide in half and stuff inside of each fish.

In a separate bowl, beat egg whites until they begin to form stiff peaks. Add the 4 cups of salt and mix thoroughly. Cover fish with salt crust to create a dome effect. You can place a layer of the salt crust under the fish as well.

Roast in oven for 20-25 minutes. Remove from oven and use a kitchen mallet to break the crust.

satsuma butter sauce

Grate and remove zest from 2 of the satsumas and peel and separate into segments. Juice the remaining satsumas. Set aside.

Melt butter in a small sauté pan over low heat for about 4 minutes, or until solids turn a nutty brown. Remove from heat and keep warm.

In a separate pan, bring juice, zest, and vinegar to a boil. Reduce heat to simmer and cook until reduced by half. Remove from heat and whisk in shallot, mustard, and green onions. Whisk in butter and oil. Continue to whisk to create an emulsion. Stir in salt, pepper, and hot sauce. Serve over fish, and garnish with satsuma segments.

TIPS & suggestions

Yes this dish works great with meats and fowl. Depending on the size of your main ingredient, simply adjust the salt crust to cover thoroughly.

Lemon-Blueberry Pound Cake

One of the best pastry chefs in America is my good friend Joe Trull. He and his wife Heidi have a place in the Carolinas that will knock your socks off. I can't tell you how many times he tried to teach me how to make a pie crust. I did eventually get it down, but mine are not as great as his. One of my favorite desserts he makes is his grandmother's pound cake recipe. Cases of beer have yet to cajole him into giving it up. If I've asked once, I've asked a million times. He just smiles because he knows it's that good. This rendition is my attempt at his perfect cake. I'll keep asking, but in the meantime, I'll rank this the number two best pound cake in the world.

Serves 10 to 12

Lemon-Blueberry Pound Cake

2 3/4 cups all-purpose flour

1 1/2 teaspoons baking powder

1/4 teaspoon baking soda

1/4 teaspoon salt

1 cup butter, softened

1 3/4 cups sugar

4 eggs

2 tablespoons lemon juice

1 tablespoon lemon zest

1 teaspoon vanilla

1 cup buttermilk

2 tablespoons all-purpose flour

2 cups blueberries

Simple Summer Cake Glaze

1 1/2 cups powdered sugar

1/8 cup freshly squeezed lemon juice

1 tablespoon corn syrup

10 whole mint leaves, optional

Lemon-Blueberry Pound Cake

Preheat oven to 350 degrees. Prepare a Bundt pan with cooking spray.

In a large mixing bowl, whisk together 2 3/4 cups flour, baking powder, baking soda, and salt. Set aside.

In a separate bowl or mixer, cream the butter. Add sugar and beat until fluffy, about 3 minutes. Add eggs, 1 at a time, mixing thoroughly before adding the next egg. Add juice, zest, and vanilla and continue to mix. Add buttermilk and flour mixture in thirds, alternating between the buttermilk and flour mixture, mixing thoroughly between additions.

Place blueberries in a medium bowl and toss with 2 tablespoons flour, to coat. Gently fold blueberries into the batter, and then fold into prepared Bundt pan.

Bake for 45–50 minutes, or until cooked through and a toothpick inserted comes out clean. Remove from oven and let cool for 30 minutes. Loosen from pan with a sharp knife and invert onto a serving plate.

SIMPLE SUMMER CAKE GLAZE

In a small mixing bowl, combine the powdered sugar, juice, and syrup; mix thoroughly until smooth and no lumps are visible.

Drizzle over top of cooled cake and garnish with mint leaves before serving.

TIPS & SUGGESTIONS

Coating the blueberries in flour is the key to keeping them dispersed throughout the batter. Skipping this step will result in the little blue nuggets sinking to the bottom of the baking pan. And my friends, you want them to be in every bite.

MOM'S DESSERTS

I love sugar. I try to say I don't, but I really do. I can't recall exactly when the change came for me. As a kid I was not a big dessert eater. I do remember getting excited around the holidays because certain dishes would appear in the kitchen. Some of those visiting dishes were Mom's yellow cake with the chocolate fudge icing, sweet potato pie, and of course the stars of the show, coconut cake and her layered fruit ambrosia.

One signal that company was coming was when Swann's cake flour appeared in the grocery basket during our Saturday shopping escapades. Swann's cake flour meant Mom was going to dive into some serious baking. She always kept Gold Medal All-Purpose flour, but I remember one of her tricks was having me sift cake flour and all-purpose flour together. She'd always have me sift the flour three times. I think it was just to keep me busy while she buzzed around.

Mom never made a white cake. I think it was the fact she had mastered the art of making a yellow cake and it became her thing. White cake seemed to be a step back for her, and because we never had it at home, I've become a connoisseur. I have to admit to traipsing all over New Orleans looking for Blue Bell's newest flavor, Bride's Cake ice cream, the epitome of white cake flavor.

Back to Mom's yellow cake, which by the way was out of sight. Top her cake with her signature coconut icing and man the memories just flow. But watch out for her chocolate fudge icing over the yellow cake, too. If you put both cakes in front of me it would be hard to choose the winner.

LAGNIAPPE

Coconut is not actually a nut. It's a drupe. What's a drupe? It's a fleshy fruit with a thin skin and a central stone containing the seed. Plums, cherries, and almonds are other examples of drupes.

Going to the trouble of cracking a fresh coconut and grating the white flesh is totally worth the effort, and I highly recommend it. Drill a hole in the coconut first to drain the water. It's delicious and nutritious.

Frozen Ambrosia

Mom's version meant that she layered all of the fruit—a layer of orange, a layer of coconut, a layer of pineapple, a layer of apples, and so on. She would dust a little bit of sugar in between. She'd build those layers to the top of the bowl and then place it in the refrigerator. It wasn't until it was out on the sideboard that she would stir it. I guess she did that to keep me and my dad away until she was ready to mix. **Serves 8 to 10**

---

1 (20-ounce) can pineapple chunks, drained

1 (11-ounce) can Mandarin oranges, drained, or fresh satsuma segments

$^1/_4$ cup maraschino cherries, drained and rinsed

$^1/_2$ cup halved red grapes

$^1/_2$ cup chopped Red Delicious apples

1 cup shaved coconut

$^1/_3$ cup toasted pecan halves

1 cup miniature marshmallows

$^1/_4$ cup sour cream

8 ounces whipped cream

In a large mixing bowl, combine the fruit, coconut, nuts, and marshmallows. Set aside.

In a separate bowl, whisk together the sour cream and whipped cream. Gently fold into fruit mixture to combine, keeping fruit pieces intact.

Place mixture in a loaf pan or ring mold and freeze until solid, about 8 hours. Loosen by running under hot water for 15 seconds then invert on a serving tray and slice and serve.

TIPS & Suggestions

Use whatever fruits you prefer. Make sure to drain the fruits that are packed in a syrup otherwise the ambrosia will be too syrupy and will melt the whipped cream. You can also just chill the fruit mixture in a covered bowl and serve without freezing.

APPLE-CREAM CHEESE SLAB PIE

All of the women in my life made some type of apple pie. All of them delicious. I'd hear people talk about slab pie. I thought okay, but can it be as great a pie as my grandma's? I thought I'd give it a go. This is a way to quickly whip out a pie, without messing with a pie crust, that will impress yourself and your friends in a short amount of time. **Serves 4 to 6**

---

4 tablespoons unsalted butter

1 pound Granny Smith apples, peeled, cored, and sliced into 1/4-inch slices

1/4 cup brown sugar

1 teaspoon ground cinnamon

1 teaspoon ground nutmeg

1 teaspoon allspice

1/4 cup cream cheese

All-purpose flour, for dusting

1 (9 x 10-inch) frozen puff pastry sheet

1 egg, beaten

1 tablespoon raw sugar

In a large sauté pan over medium-high heat, melt butter. Add apple slices and sauté until lightly browned, 5-7 minutes. Stir in brown sugar and spices, reduce heat, and continue to sauté until apples are caramelized and softened, about 5 minutes. Add cream cheese, and mix well.

Preheat oven to 425 degrees.

Lay out a 15-inch square piece of unwaxed parchment paper and dust with flour. Place the pastry sheet on the parchment. Using a rolling pin, flatten pastry dough out slightly to extend thicker ends. Using a paring knife, split dough in half, being careful not to cut parchment.

Top one half of dough with sautéed apple mixture. Place second piece of dough on top and pinch sides and ends to seal. Brush top with egg. Make 5 slits about 1 1/2 inches long down the pastry to vent. Sprinkle generously with sugar.

Transfer pastry on parchment to baking sheet and bake for 15-17 minutes, or until golden brown. Remove and serve.

TIPS & SUGGESTIONS

Use pears, peaches, or sweet potatoes with the same outstanding results. Cinnamon, nutmeg, and allspice will work with all three.

COCONUT CAKE WITH ICING à la Lorna

You really knew it was the holidays, Thanksgiving and Christmas, because on the cake plate sat this huge white ball of glistening coconut crusted cake that looked like fresh snow. My Mom's coconut cake was the ultimate dessert. She always grated the fresh coconut, never used bagged. With this recipe, I've simplified it a bit and put some of the frosting between the layers. Mom's version was with a simple syrup that she would make and simply brush the layers, even brushing the undersides of the layers, then top with a light dusting of fresh shredded coconut. After a few days, if there was any cake left, the syrup would start to crystalize and give it a bit of a crunch. I learned to stash a slice away, well-hidden, and wait for five days to taste the glorious results of Mom's efforts. This was by far my cousin Lorna's favorite dessert that Mom made. Not a holiday goes by without her talking about this cake.
Serves 10 to 12

Cake

5 eggs

1 cup unsalted butter

1 cup whole milk

3 cups sifted cake flour

1 tablespoon baking powder

1/2 teaspoon kosher salt

2 cups sugar

1 tablespoon vanilla

1 fresh coconut, husk and peel removed, finely grated or shredded, 3 to 4 cups

Icing à la Lorna

3 egg whites

2 cups sugar

1/4 teaspoon cream of tartar

3/4 cup water

1/4 teaspoon kosher salt

2 teaspoons vanilla

Cake

Preheat oven to 350 degrees. Butter 3 (8-inch) round cake pans and line bottoms with parchment paper. Butter parchment paper, lightly dust with flour, and set aside. Let eggs, butter, and milk set at room temperature for 30 minutes.

In a medium bowl, combine flour, baking powder, and salt.

Using a mixer, beat butter on medium speed for 30 seconds. Add sugar and vanilla; beat 3-4 minutes on medium until well-combined. Add eggs, 1 at a time, beating well after each addition. Alternately add flour mixture and milk to butter mixture, beating on low after each addition, until just combined. Batter should be smooth. Divide batter evenly among the 3 pans.

Continued

Bake 20-25 minutes, or until tops spring back when lightly touched. Cool layers in pans on wire racks for 10 minutes. Remove the cake layers from pans, peel off parchment paper, and completely cool on wire racks.

Icing à la Lorna

Let egg whites stand at room temperature for 30 minutes.

Combine sugar, cream of tartar, and water in a medium saucepan. Cook and stir over low heat until sugar is dissolved. Bring to a boil, and using a candy thermometer, cook, without stirring, until temperature reaches 240 degrees (5-10 minutes).

Beat egg whites on medium-high speed until frothy. Add salt and beat just until stiff peaks begin to form. With the mixer running on low, slowly pour in hot syrup. Beat in vanilla. Increase speed to medium high and beat until light and fluffy and holds its shape, 3-4 minutes.

Place first cake layer on a serving plate. Spread the top with frosting then sprinkle generously with coconut. Stack the second and third layers of cake on the first layer, frosting and sprinkling with coconut between layers. If frosting starts to thicken, place over a bowl of hot water. When cake is completely frosted, heap with additional coconut, pressing gently with your fingers to bed the coconut.

TIPS & SUGGESTIONS

To prepare the coconut, make holes in two of the eyes with an ice pick or nut pick using a pressing, twisting motion. Pour the coconut water into a measuring cup. Crack the shell by holding the coconut in one hand while using a hammer with the other hand to firmly tap the coconut. Rotate the shell as you strike it. Separate the coconut into pieces, tapping with hammer as necessary. To remove the coconut meat, work a thin-blade knife between coconut and shell. With vegetable peeler remove brown skin from coconut, and shred using smallest holes on box grater.

Make the simple syrup and try the drizzle like my mother. Two parts sugar and one part water will make your syrup on the stove. Just heat and stir until sugar dissolves and begins to boil. Turn off the heat and cool thoroughly. Refrigerate for up to 1 week. Use leftovers to sweeten ice tea or coffee.

EGGPLANT

Eggplant is one of those ingredients that looks totally different from how it feels and tastes. I've been stymied by eggplant since I was a kid. The peel is so shiny purple, but that color goes away with cooking. Peel and slice it and it is fresh and it's spongy. Bite into it and it really has no taste. Cook it, and it becomes soft, tender, and sweet and melts in your mouth. I'm simply baffled.

You can chop it, dice it, julienne it. You can peel it, slice it, and even hollow it out. You can bake it, fry it, sauté it, and smother it down in red gravy. What I haven't had a chance to do yet is make a soup or bake it into a bread. But trust me, that's on my list.

Eggplant has such a depth of great vegetable flavor, and I find it incredibly easy to work with. I know some people can be intimidated by its size, but to me that just means picking one large eggplant and you're covered for the main ingredient in your dish.

In the Southern part of the United States, eggplant is part of our soul food cuisine. The same can be said for many world cuisines. Eggplant is grown pretty much all over the world, with the main difference between varieties being size and the color of the skin. In New Orleans, eggplant is always available, and that meant that the Italian, Chinese, Spanish, Middle Eastern, and African immigrants could actually recreate their signature dishes, which have become a part of the New Orleans culinary landscape. I believe that's why New Orleans is such a great culinary city. We have the people and resources, including ingredients, to offer such a wide expression of culture.

LAGNIAPPE

Garlic, a close relative to onions, shallots, leeks, and chives, is an essential in every Creole pantry. Typically Creole cooks add the garlic after sautéing the trinity: onion, celery, and bell pepper. Chopping, crushing, or pressing the garlic right before cooking allows the enzyme alliinase to be exposed to oxygen and convert to allicin, which then releases that fragrant, pungent garlic aroma.

Fried Eggplant Fingers with Red Gravy

When it comes to frying food, New Orleanians know how to coax the crisp and crunch from any ingredient we batter or bread. When it comes to eggplant, it's hard to think of another ingredient that not only holds up to the frying, but is actually improved by developing a flavor under the high heat of frying. Since eggplant tends to adapt by being a great vehicle for whatever it's seasoned with, it's the flavors of the batter, especially the cheese, that makes this eggplant dish one of my favorites. **Serves 4**

Eggplant

1 large eggplant (about 1 pound), peeled and cut in $1/4$-inch sticks

$1/2$ cup all-purpose flour

2 eggs, beaten

$3/4$ cup Italian breadcrumbs

$1/2$ cup grated Parmesan cheese

2 teaspoons Creole seasoning

Salt and pepper, to taste

3 to 4 cups vegetable oil

Red Gravy

1 tablespoon vegetable oil

4 cloves garlic, chopped

$1/8$ cup roughly chopped fresh basil leaves

1 tablespoon fresh oregano leaves

1 teaspoon freshly cracked pepper

$1/2$ cup tomato paste

3 large tomatoes, chopped and seeds removed

1 teaspoon kosher salt

$1/8$ cup vegetable stock, as needed

Eggplant

Preheat oven to 425 degrees.

Place the flour in a shallow bowl. In a separate shallow bowl, add the eggs, and then combine the breadcrumbs, cheese, Creole seasoning, and salt and pepper together in a third shallow bowl.

Heat oil in skillet to 350 degrees.

Working in batches, coat eggplant pieces with flour, dip in egg wash, and then coat with breadcrumb mixture. Fry in oil 3–5 minutes, turning once if needed, until golden brown. Remove and drain on paper towels. Serve with Red Gravy.

Red Gravy

Heat oil on medium-high heat. Sauté garlic for 2 minutes. Add basil, oregano, and pepper and sauté for 1 minute. Add tomato paste and sauté for 1 minute. Add tomatoes and salt; stir to break up pieces. Bring to a boil and reduce to a simmer. Cover, and let sauce simmer on low heat for 15 minutes, stirring occasionally. Add stock to achieve a thinner sauce if that is preferred.

TIPS & SUGGESTIONS

Not big into frying? Just bake in a preheated
oven at 425 degrees, on a baking sheet until
golden brown.

Eggplant Napoleon

Sometimes you just want a great tasting vegetable dish. The mild flavor of zucchini and squash is highlighted by the red onion and eggplant. It looks so pretty on the plate with the thick-sliced eggplant taking the lead in this dish. These little individual delicacies are a perfect side dish or are great as a main entrée. **Serves 4**

---

1 large eggplant (about 1 pound), cut in $1/4$-inch-thick slices

Kosher salt, for sprinkling

$1/2$ cup safflower oil, divided

4 large Creole tomatoes, sliced into $1/4$-inch-thick rounds

2 medium red onions, cut in $1/4$-inch-thick rounds

1 large zucchini, cut in $1/4$-inch-thick rounds

1 large yellow squash, cut in $1/4$-inch-thick rounds

$3/4$ cup ricotta cheese

2 teaspoons Creole seasoning

$1/4$ cup Italian breadcrumbs

$1/4$ cup grated mozzarella cheese

Preheat oven to 425 degrees.

Place eggplant slices in a single layer on a large baking sheet and sprinkle with salt. Let stand for 10 minutes until eggplant begins to sweat. Using a paper towel, pat eggplant slices dry. Brush tops lightly with oil. Place in oven and roast for 15 minutes. Remove and cool to room temperature.

Arrange the tomatoes, onions, zucchini, and squash on a separate baking sheet and brush lightly with oil. Place in oven and roast for 10 minutes. Remove and cool to room temperature.

Mix ricotta cheese and Creole seasoning in a small mixing bowl.

Line a clean baking sheet with parchment paper and arrange the vegetables as follows: eggplant, thin coating of cheese mixture, tomato, onion, eggplant, thin coating of cheese mixture, zucchini, squash, eggplant, cheese mixture. Sprinkle tops with breadcrumbs and mozzarella cheese. Bake for 20–25 minutes, or until golden brown. Serve warm.

TIPS & Suggestions

Add crabmeat, shrimp, or even slices of prosciutto in between the layers to add more power, and serve with a summer salad for a fresh New Orleans dinner.

EGGPLaNT PirOGUE

I had my first eggplant pirogue at K-Paul's Louisiana Kitchen, the wonderful Chef Paul Prudhomme's home base in New Orleans. The flavor of the seafood and eggplant together . . . now that's how you eat your vegetables. **Serves 4**

---

2 large eggplants

Kosher salt and pepper to taste

1 1/2 cups fine seasoned breadcrumbs, or fine cornmeal

3 tablespoons Creole seasoning

1 cup all-purpose flour

2 eggs, beaten

Vegetable oil

3 tablespoons salted butter

1 tablespoon minced garlic

2 tablespoons chopped shallot

1/4 cup cream

2 pounds lobster tails, chopped

2 tablespoons lemon juice

2 tablespoons chopped parsley

2 tablespoons chopped chives

Prepare eggplants by removing skin and cutting in half. Scoop out the seeds, leaving behind about 1/2 inch of flesh. Cut a thin slice off the bottom of each half to create a flat bottom, giving the eggplant halves a classic boat shape. Season with salt and pepper.

Combine the breadcrumbs and Creole seasoning together in a small bowl. Dust a fine layer of flour over the entire eggplant halves. Dip in egg wash and coat with breading.

Heat oil to 350 degrees in a deep fryer or large Dutch oven.

Place breaded eggplant halves in hot oil and fry until golden brown, about 5 minutes. Turn several times during frying to cook evenly.

In a large skillet, heat butter and add garlic and shallot, sauté for 3 minutes. Add cream, stir well and add lobster, cook for 5 minutes. Reduce heat and add lemon juice, parsley, and chives. Remove from heat and spoon into the Eggplant Pirogue.

TIPS & SUGGESTIONS

It's easy to make these boat-shaped eggplants. But if you are in a hurry or don't have a deep fryer, just thick slice the eggplant, about a good inch thick and fry. Then assemble on a plate by topping with the creamy seafood. Less drama but just as good.

GREEK

I was in high school when I first noticed a festival behind a church on Bayou St. John. Greek flags were flying everywhere on the bayou, celebrating the culture of those folks who established the Holy Trinity Greek Orthodox Cathedral in 1864. For years and years I would tell myself I needed to get over there and experience the food and the music. My friends went, but somehow, I just did not make it.

In 2002 I was out and about over Memorial Day weekend and passed the church. Someone pulled out of a parking place right near the entrance as I passed by. I took that as a sign to just stop and go. People park for blocks and blocks to experience the Greek Festival. So I'm there, I'm thrilled, and I've got VIP parking.

As soon as I walked in, I saw people I knew all over the place, all telling me to try the lamb. Behind tables situated on the lawn, rotisserie roasted lamb was being sliced and served on fresh pita and topped with tzatziki, onion, lettuce, and tomato. And there were lamb burgers. I had to pace myself. As I was walking, someone stopped me and said, "Chef, have you been inside?"

As I made my way inside the hall, the culinary angels sang. Lined end to end were tables filled with desserts from one side of the hall to the other. I recognized the baklava, but many of the gems were traditional Greek desserts I have never heard of. I picked four of everything, knowing I had to share with Jonathan and Kevin.

I left there with three cake boxes filled with Greek delicacies.

I also left with a couple of to-go plates full of things like moussaka, stuffed grape leaves, salad, and Greek meat balls. The community spirit behind there was inspiring. That food to the members of the church was such an honest expression of the soul of their culture. I left with a full stomach, a full heart, and a full appreciation for my fellow New Orleanians. The annual Greek Festival keeps us all up to snuff on what it means to be Greek. It's the music, the food, and the community, just like New Orleans herself.

LAGNIAPPE

True Greek-style yogurt is a cultural flavor marker that is universally understood to be authentically Greek. The process of cooking basic yogurt is fascinating. The recipe is pretty simple. Milk from a cow or sheep is slowly heated to 160 degrees, and then cooled to 110 degrees before adding yogurt cultures, either lactobacillus bulgaricus or streptococcus thermophilus. After introducing the living bacteria, the 110-degree temperature is maintained from 5 hours to as long as 10 hours. The yogurt is then strained three times to remove most of the liquid, resulting in the thick, sweet and tart culinary creation we have come to know and love.

CHICKEN SOUVLAKI AND TZATZIKI

Certain dishes can be intimidating until you realize that it has a culinary companion in a dish you are already familiar with. This is basically chicken and veggies on a skewer. How much more American can you get? But remember, we are going Greek here. What makes this dish special and extraordinary is the yogurt-based sauce. **Serves 4**

CHICKEN SOUVLAKI

3 tablespoons freshly squeezed lemon juice

1 1/2 teaspoons chopped fresh oregano

2 teaspoons olive oil

1/2 teaspoon kosher salt

4 cloves garlic, minced

1/2 pound boneless, skinless chicken breasts, cut in 1-inch pieces

1 zucchini, cut into 1/2-inch-thick pieces

Wooden skewers, soaked in water

TZATZIKI SAUCE

1/2 cup peeled, grated, and seeded cucumber

1/2 cup thick Greek yogurt, or plain or low fat yogurt

1 tablespoon lemon juice

2 teaspoons chopped fresh dill

1/4 teaspoon kosher salt

1 clove garlic, minced

CHICKEN SOUVLAKI

Combine the lemon juice, oregano, oil, salt, and garlic in a large ziplock bag, seal and shake to combine. Add chicken, seal bag, and toss to coat. Place in refrigerator and marinate for 1 hour.

Remove chicken from marinade and thread pieces on the skewers, alternating with zucchini.

Heat a griddle pan to sizzling. Add skewers and cook until chicken is done, about 8 minutes. Turn during cooking to ensure the chicken is cooked on all sides.

TZATZIKI SAUCE

Combine all ingredients and lightly process in a blender to achieve a smooth consistency. Cover and chill. Serve with souvlaki as a dipping sauce.

TIPS & SUGGESTIONS

I like to make my chicken skewers from dark meat found on the thighs. Pork, lamb, or beef are also traditional souvlaki ingredients.

MOUSSaKa

This reminds me of the shepherd's pie that our Irish New Orleanians make, but only in the construction. It's topped with eggplant and béchamel sauce. It's easy to assemble and bake in one dish. **Serves 4**

1/4 cup olive oil

2 pounds ground beef

1 small onion, finely chopped

15 ounces tomato sauce

3/4 cup dry red wine

2 tablespoons chopped fresh parsley

1 tablespoon chopped fresh oregano

1/4 teaspoon ground cinnamon

1 large eggplant, about 1 1/2 pounds, peeled and cut into 1/4-inch-thick slices

BéCHaMeL Sauce

4 tablespoons butter

1/4 cup all-purpose flour

2 cups whole milk

3 eggs, beaten

1 cup grated Parmesan cheese, divided

Kosher salt and freshly cracked pepper, to taste

Preheat oven to 350 degrees.

In a large saucepan, heat oil on medium-high heat. Sauté beef and onion until beef is crumbled and browned, about 15 minutes. Add tomato sauce, wine, parsley, oregano, and cinnamon. Simmer until mixture thickens and cooks down, about 20 minutes.

BéCHaMeL

In a heavy-bottom saucepan over medium heat, melt butter. Slowly add flour and stir to combine. Gradually whisk in milk to a smooth consistency. Bring to a boil, stirring constantly. Remove from heat and add 1/3 of the eggs, whisking constantly. Add another 1/3 of the eggs while continuing to whisk. Once combined, add the last of the eggs.

Return saucepan to heat and bring to a boil, continuing to whisk as sauce thickens. Stir in 1/2 of the cheese. Season with salt and pepper.

In a 9 x 12-inch glass baking dish, layer half of the eggplant slices evenly in the bottom; season with salt and pepper. Add the beef mixture and top with remaining eggplant. Pour hot béchamel evenly over the eggplant and cover with remaining cheese.

Cover loosely with aluminum foil and bake for 50 minutes. Remove foil and bake until bubbling and browned on edges, 10-15 minutes. Serve warm.

TIPS & SUggesTIONS

This recipe calls for ground beef, but ground lamb is also traditional. I've made this dish with ground turkey and bison and it's sensational. If you want to use pork, just drain off the fat after sautéing before adding the rest of the ingredients.

Baklava

I remember the first time I encountered baklava. With all the chopped nuts in it, I thought it was a meat pie. After taking my first bite, I was looking for a strong cup of coffee. And I was hooked. **Serves 8 to 10**

---

1 cup butter, softened plus extra for buttering pan

1 pound chopped nuts, walnuts are traditional

1 teaspoon ground cinnamon

1 (16-ounce) package frozen phyllo dough, thawed

1 cup sugar

1 cup filtered water

1 teaspoon vanilla

1/2 cup honey

Preheat oven to 350 degrees. Prepare a 9 x 12-inch baking pan by buttering sides and bottom.

In a medium bowl, toss nuts with cinnamon to thoroughly coat.

Working quickly, unroll dough and trim to fit in the pan. Place a very damp cloth over dough to keep moist while you work.

Start with a layer of 3 phyllo sheets and place in baking pan. Butter the top. Lightly sprinkle 3 tablespoons of the nut mixture evenly over the buttered dough. Top with 3 more sheets of phyllo, butter, and add nuts. Repeat the process until you have built 8 layers. Finish with a layer of buttered phyllo.

Using a very sharp knife, cut into diagonals or squares before putting it into the oven. Place in oven and bake, uncovered, until golden and crisp, 45–50 minutes.

In a small saucepan, boil the sugar and water until sugar dissolves, about 5 minutes. Add vanilla and honey and simmer for about 15 minutes.

Remove baklava from oven and gently spoon honey sauce over the top to coat and soak through the layers. Let cool and serve.

TIPS & SUGGESTIONS

You must cut the phyllo dough before baking, because once baked, you can't cut it. Of course that's alright by me. I'll take the first piece, but that means nobody else gets any!

THE BERRY BEST

I learned from Mom how to appreciate the ingredients that come not only from New Orleans, but from all over Louisiana. She loved berries in particular. Especially the ones that came from the North Shore, right across Lake Pontchartrain and about 35 minutes from downtown. Strawberries, blueberries, and blackberries were her favorites. In season, the blueberries and blackberries were always in the refrigerator in her berry bowl for all of us to snack on. The strawberries, however, would get a different treatment.

Mom would remove the stem and slice the strawberries almost paper thin. She put those thin slices in a bowl and sprinkled just the slightest bit of sugar over them. Then another layer and same, a sprinkle of sugar. Those strawberries would be sealed with plastic wrap and placed in the fridge. I was given, along with my Dad, a strict order to stay out. As the berries set, the sugar drew out the juices. Southern magic.

My Dad, being a huge dessert fan, loved Mom's pound cake with those sugared strawberries. As a child, I remember my first taste of the strawberry juice. Mom delicately spooned out a bit of the bright red liquid for me to savor. And boy, I can remember thinking it was pure culinary genius.

My first blueberry memory is of a pancake drizzled with cane syrup and topped with those little blue nuggets. I can tell you I've been hooked on blueberries ever since. Still to this day, I always have a cup of fruit with berries for breakfast.

LAGNIAPPE

Just outside of New Orleans and across Lake Pontchartrain in Tangipahoa and Livingston Parishes, growers begin planting strawberries at the end of September through early October. The more than eighty-five growers in and around those two parishes will begin harvesting the red fruit gems around the holidays and continue through the peak of the season in March and April, culminating with the Ponchatoula Strawberry Festival. Ponchatoula, a town of about 5000 people, welcomes more than 25,000 visitors to this annual celebration of the Louisiana strawberry. Louisiana is always a top ten producer of strawberries in the United States. Strawberries are so ingrained in our culinary culture, that in 2001 the state of Louisiana named the strawberry the official state fruit.

Pecan-Stuffed French Toast

My favorite place to have stuffed French toast was at Elizabeth's in the Bywater when Chef Heidi was first getting started in New Orleans with her landmark restaurant. As a matter of fact, this was the first time I had anything remotely resembling a "stuffed" pain perdu or "lost bread." Mom made this dish, but stopped short of where Heidi really got my attention. She sliced the French bread on the bias and put huge amounts of fruit and cream and syrup all over the plate and in between the bread. Heaven. It was like my Mom's version, but Heidi took it to the next level. **Serves 8**

---

16 ounces cream cheese, softened and whipped

1 cup chopped pecans, divided

16 slices brioche

6 eggs

1 cup heavy cream

1 teaspoon ground cinnamon

1 teaspoon vanilla

1 tablespoon sugar

1/8 teaspoon salt

2 tablespoons butter, plus more as needed

Steen's syrup or maple syrup

1/2 cup blueberries

1/2 cup raspberries

1 cup strawberries, sliced

Preheat oven to 200 degrees.

In a small bowl, combine cream cheese and 1/2 cup pecans. Divide and spread cream cheese mixture evenly over 8 slices of bread and then top each slice with remaining bread to form a sandwich.

In a large bowl, beat eggs with cream, cinnamon, vanilla, sugar, and salt to make a thin batter. Dip each sandwich in the batter to lightly coat.

Melt butter in a skillet or griddle over medium heat and fry sandwiches until golden brown on both sides. Add more butter to the skillet as needed. Place finished French toast sandwiches in the oven to keep warm while you fry the others.

To serve, plate each French toast sandwich and sprinkle remaining pecans evenly over the tops; drizzle with syrup and top with blueberries, raspberries, and strawberries.

Tips & Suggestions

Any bread works. Be sure to use bread that's a few days old. It just holds up better.

STUFFED PORK CHOPS WITH BACON-MAPLE REDUCTION

Often Mom would just fry pork chops; super simple. I remember the day she came home with these huge, double-cut pork chops. I was enthralled and excited to see what she did with them. I don't remember exactly what she stuffed those chops with, but she hollowed out that little pocket and filled them up. It was like a savory stuffed pork chop sandwich but without the bread. Just fantastic. I love this cut on a pork chop. They just look great on the plate. **Serves 4**

STUFFED PORK CHOPS

4 thick cut, bone in pork chops

4 tablespoons butter

3 pears, diced

3/4 cup diced onion

1 tablespoon rosemary

1 tablespoon oil

3 tablespoons Creole seasoning

BACON-MAPLE REDUCTION

4 slices thick cut bacon

1 pear, diced

1 clove garlic, minced

1 cup apple juice

1/2 cup pure maple syrup

1/4 cup dried cranberries

STUFFED PORK CHOPS

Preheat oven to 350 degrees.

Rinse and pat pork chops dry. Using a paring knife, slice pork chops lengthwise to make a pocket.

In a medium saucepan, melt butter and add pears and onion; stir and cook for 5 minutes. Add rosemary and cook for 2 minutes. Remove from heat, divide evenly between chops and stuff in pockets. Place chops in a baking dish, drizzle with oil, and sprinkle with seasoning. Bake for 40 minutes, or until pork chops reach a minimum temperature of 145 degrees. Allow to rest for at least 3 minutes before serving.

BACON-MAPLE REDUCTION

In a sauté pan, cook bacon slices until crispy. Remove from pan and let drain on paper towels. Crumble when cooled; set aside. Discard grease.

In the same pan, sauté pear and garlic until golden brown, about 1 minute. Deglaze the pan with the apple juice then add the maple syrup and cranberries. Cook to reduce the liquid by half. If you would like the sauce to be thicker, continue cooking it down until it reaches desired consistency. Remember it will thicken as it sits. Remove from heat and add the bacon to the sauce and drizzle over the pork.

TIPS & SUGGESTIONS

If the double cut chop isn't readily available at your supermarket, or you just want to buy the family pack, you can stuff them by layering.

Start with a thin chop, add a couple of table-spoons of the stuffing, and top with another chop. Secure with a couple of toothpicks and you've got yourself an easy rendition.

Lemon Biscuit "Shortcake" with Mixed Berries

When the Ponchatoula strawberries come into season along with the rest of our berry harvest, we are flush with these locally grown jewels until at least the start of the summer weather. And with the berry harvest comes berry shortcake. I'm crazy for this dessert and order it wherever I go. Quite often, however, the spongy cake that the berries rest on with the traditional juice and cream topping just doesn't hold up. I always feel as though the cake needs to be less absorbent and that a southern-style biscuit might better fit the bill. So that is what I've done with this recipe. The lemon essence of the biscuit gives a slight enhancement to the ripe berries and compliments the dish like sunshine and summer. **Serves 8 to 10**

LEMON BISCUITS

1 package active dry yeast

$1/2$ cup warm water

2 cups whole milk

Juice and zest of 1 lemon

5 cups all-purpose flour

$1/4$ cup sugar

1 teaspoon baking powder

1 teaspoon baking soda

1 teaspoon kosher salt

$1/2$ cup unsalted butter, cubed and chilled

MIXED BERRIES

1 pint fresh strawberries, sliced

1 pint fresh blueberries

1 pint fresh blackberries

1 pint fresh raspberries

$1/4$ cup sugar

2 tablespoons freshly squeezed lemon juice

1 teaspoon lemon zest

LEMON BISCUITS

Combine yeast with warm water and stir to dissolve. In a small bowl, combine the milk and lemon juice. Allow to set for 15 minutes at room temperature to curdle.

In a large mixing bowl, whisk together the flour, sugar, baking powder, baking soda, and salt. Add zest and mix with hands to allow zest to evenly release oils.

Add the butter, and using your fingers, work butter into flour mixture until mixture is crumbly. Add yeast mixture and milk. Stir to just moisten. Cover tightly and refrigerate to allow yeast and dough to rise, at least 2 hours or overnight.

Preheat oven to 450 degrees.

Turn out the dough on a generously floured surface. Knead lightly until dough is smooth enough to pat out easily, being careful not to over work the

dough. Cut out biscuit rounds using a cookie cutter or glass.

Place biscuits on an ungreased baking sheet and bake until golden, about 12 minutes. Remove from oven and cool on a wire rack.

MIXED BERRIES

Place the berries in a large mixing bowl, and sprinkle in the sugar, juice, and zest; mix gently.

Cover and chill in the refrigerator and allow fruit to macerate.

To serve, slice biscuits in half and spoon berries over the bottoms. Add biscuit tops to the berries at an angle, or place berries on both halves.

TIPS & SUGGESTIONS

Add a scoop of vanilla ice scream on top of all of this. Makes the shortcake wondrous. Watch yourself!

MOM'S NIGHT OUT

I loved going out to dinner with Mom and Aunt Dorothy. That meant watching my two favorite ladies being served and treated the way they took care of all of us every day.

You see at the house, ours and Aunt Dorothy's, they would serve all of us first before they even thought about sitting down and eating. As a matter of fact, during the holidays when Mom, Dad, and Nan hosted everyone else, I never remember Mom sitting at the table. I guess she picked and ate while she prepared everything. You could invite her, and pull out a chair, but there was no way she was sitting down. She was too busy making sure that plates were full and we all got a taste of everything. Aunt Dorothy was the same.

All of us guys, Dad, Uncle Chet, and Cousin Chet along with my cousin Lorna, were so blessed to have had Mom, Dorothy, and Nan taking care of all of us in every way. They fed our minds, they fed our bodies, and they fed our souls.

When we went to Dooky Chase's, we sat together at a big family table. That's the restaurant I remember us going to pretty often. My Mom really loved Chef Leah's cooking. I was always at the far end of the table with Chet. I can still see my Mom laughing, talking, and smiling with the people I love the most. She would always glance in my direction to make sure I was acting right, and most importantly, getting enough to eat.

LAGNIAPPE

A well-seasoned cast iron pan is a necessity for any kitchen, professional or home. It's simple to season a cast iron pan. If it's brand new, just rinse with soapy water. If it's used, brush vigorously with steel wool or a steel brush and clean with mild, soapy water. In both instances rinse thoroughly. Immediately place on the stovetop on high heat and allow the heat to first dry any remaining moisture and continue to heat until extremely hot. Add a few tablespoons of high heat oil such as vegetable oil, swipe to thoroughly coat the inside of the pan using a thick kitchen towel or paper towels, remove from heat, and allow the pan to cool. Once the skillet is seasoned, avoid washing with soapy water. The soap will break down the seasoned coating which is composed of tiny molecules that actually make the cast iron nonstick.

Beef TournedoS WITH PeTITe TWICe-BaKeD POTaToeS

Mom never really cooked a lot of steaks at home. She had so many seafood and New Orleans-style recipes in her repertoire that I believe she left the steak cooking up to the restaurant chefs. It was a treat for her to go out and order steak. She usually ordered petite cuts of meat, and these medallions would have been right up her alley. ***Serves 4***

Beef FILeTS

4 (6-ounce) beef filets, cut into 3 ounce medallions

Kosher salt and freshly cracked pepper, to taste

1 tablespoon butter

1 pound baby portobello mushrooms, quartered

2 shallots, minced

1 cup dry red wine

2 tablespoons Creole or Dijon mustard

2 tablespoons cold unsalted butter

4 ounces goat cheese

PeTITe TWICe-BaKeD POTaToeS

20 fingerling potatoes

2 tablespoons vegetable oil, plus extra to coat

4 ounces thick-cut bacon, cooked crisp and crumbled

2 teaspoons fresh thyme leaves

$1/8$ cup finely chopped fresh chives

$1/2$ cup sour cream

Kosher salt and pepper, to taste

$1/2$ cup grated fresh Parmesan cheese

Beef FILeTS

Preheat oven to 200 degrees.

Season filets with salt and pepper. Heat 1 tablespoon of butter in a cast iron skillet over medium-high heat. Add seasoned filets and cook until medium rare, about 4 minutes per side. Remove from skillet and place on a heat proof plate and place in oven to keep warm.

Add mushrooms and shallots to same skillet and sauté until shallots are translucent, about 2 minutes. Deglaze skillet with wine and scrape all drippings and pieces from bottom with a wooden spoon. Bring to a boil and simmer until reduced by half. Stir in mustard and cold butter to fully incorporate.

To serve, assemble tournedos in layers on each plate first with a filet, then goat cheese, and another filet. Top with sauce and serve hot.

Continued

PETITE TWICE-BAKED POTATOES

Preheat oven to 425 degrees.

Pierce each potato with a fork and coat with a thin layer of oil. Arrange potatoes on a baking sheet and bake for 20-25 minutes, or until tender.

Remove from oven and cool for 20 minutes, or until they can easily be handled. Slice potatoes and place in a large bowl. Add the bacon, thyme, chives, sour cream, salt, and pepper. Mix well.

Coat a 9-inch square baking dish with oil. Add potato mixture, and spread to cover bottom of dish. Top with cheese and bake until heated through, about 7 minutes. Serve hot.

TIPS & SUGGESTIONS

This recipe calls for goat cheese, but you can use blue cheese, too.

Fried Chicken with Honey Drizzle

Mom could fry some chicken. She was also a curious culinarian, and she loved to taste and compare what chefs at some of her favorite restaurants passed off as a great fried chicken. But you know after all that taste testing, she stayed true to her recipe. I'm thankful for that because my mother made the best fried chicken I've ever tasted. Since I really love sweet and savory together, I like to drizzle the honey and lemon over Mom's fried chicken recipe to get my fix. **Serves 4**

Fried Chicken

2 tablespoons garlic powder

1 tablespoon onion powder

2 tablespoons salt, divided

2 tablespoons white pepper, divided

1 teaspoon cayenne pepper

4 tablespoons Creole seasoning, divided

1 whole chicken, cut in pieces

2 cups flour

Honey Drizzle

1/2 cup honey

Juice of 1 lemon

1/4 cup chopped parsley

Fried Chicken

In a large bowl combine the garlic powder, onion powder, 1 tablespoon salt, 1 tablespoon white pepper, cayenne pepper, and 2 tablespoons Creole seasoning. Add the chicken, and toss to coat each piece thoroughly. Place in a covered container and refrigerate for 4 hours or overnight.

Mix flour, remaining salt, white pepper, and Creole seasoning in a large bowl.

Heat oil to 365 degrees in deep fryer.

Remove chicken from refrigerator and dredge each piece in seasoned flour, shaking off excess.

Place coated chicken pieces in hot oil and fry for 12–15 minutes, or until chicken juices runs clear.

Honey Drizzle

In a small bowl, stir together the honey and lemon juice. Drizzle over fried chicken and sprinkle with parsley, to serve.

Tips & Suggestions

The addition of 2 tablespoons of hot sauce to the honey and lemon juice will elevate the flavor even more.

Baked corn on the cob with Honey Butter

When my mom pulled out the little yellow corn-on-the-cob holders, I was beside myself knowing that she had bought fresh corn from the vegetable vendor who came by the house on Wednesday evening and Saturday morning. She baked them to keep that sweet flavor that often times can be boiled out of the kernels. **Serves 4**

Baked corn

4 fresh cobs corn, silk removed, rinsed and patted dry

4 tablespoons butter, softened

2 teaspoons kosher salt

1 teaspoon pepper

3 tablespoons minced fresh parsley

1 teaspoon sweet Spanish paprika

1 teaspoon Creole seasoning

Salt and pepper, to taste

Honey Butter

2 cups butter, room temperature

1/4 cup honey

1/2 teaspoon vanilla

1/2 teaspoon cayenne pepper

Baked corn

Preheat oven to 375 degrees.

Break corn cobs in half and arrange in a large roasting pan.

In a small mixing bowl, combine the butter, salt, pepper, parsley, paprika, and Creole seasoning. Divide mixture evenly among the corn pieces, smearing to coat. Seal pan tightly with a lid or aluminum foil.

Bake for 10 minutes, or until corn is tender. Remove and serve with salt and pepper and a slice of Honey Butter.

Honey Butter

In mixer bowl on low speed, combine the butter, honey, vanilla, and cayenne. Mix for 3 minutes to incorporate. Spoon the butter onto a piece of plastic wrap and shape into a log. Cover with plastic and twist ends tight. Chill in refrigerator until firm. Cut into slices to serve.

TIPS & Suggestions

If you don't have room in the oven and have to boil the cobs, bring the water to a boil and add 1 tablespoon of salt. Place the shucked cobs in the water and return the water to a boil. Only boil for about 3 minutes and then turn off the heat. Let them sit for another 5 minutes, drain, and serve hot.

INDEX

METRIC CONVERSION CHART

Volume Measurements		Weight Measurements		Temperature Conversion	
U.S.	Metric	U.S.	Metric	Fahrenheit	Celsius
1 teaspoon	5 ml	½ ounce	15 g	250	120
1 tablespoon	15 ml	1 ounce	30 g	300	150
¼ cup	60 ml	3 ounces	90 g	325	160
⅓ cup	75 ml	4 ounces	115 g	350	180
½ cup	125 ml	8 ounces	225 g	375	190
⅔ cup	150 ml	12 ounces	350 g	400	200
¾ cup	175 ml	1 pound	450 g	425	220
1 cup	250 ml	2¼ pounds	1 kg	450	230

ACKNOWLEDGMENTS

I am a very fortunate man to be surrounded by such great people.

Rhonda Findley, my coauthor, can peel me like an onion and get to my core to tease out the stories like no one else. Monica Pazmino is not only my business partner and my life partner, but she is, most importantly, my best friend who makes me the best person I can be.

I am also lucky to work with an enormously talented producer and crew at two of New Orleans' premier TV stations, WYES, our New Orleans PBS station, and WWL-TV, our CBS affiliate.

My kitchen staff Austin, Cabral, and David, you are so very much appreciated.

Eugenia Uhl, whose photographs make me want to lick every picture in the book because they make me remember how good it all tasted.

To New Orleans, the people, the places, and the beautiful spirit that has been passed down from generation to generation for 300 years. Happy Birthday to our magnificent city!

To my dear friend Gibbs Smith, and the entire Gibbs Smith family, especially Michelle Branson, who has not only been my editor through this process, but who has also become a good friend.

And to you—thank you for letting me share my life with you through these pages of stories and recipes.

-Kevin

Spending three hundred hours with Chef Kevin putting together his thoughts, memories, and recipes is only fitting as we here in New Orleans are celebrating the 300th anniversary of one of the greatest culinary cities in the world. Sharing time with Kevin has made me a true New Orleanian, and for that I will forever be grateful. It is an honor to be trusted by such an extraordinary person and culinarian. Bringing his vision to life is an experience I will never forget. It is always difficult to find the best words to really thank you, Chef Kevin, for allowing me this honor. So maybe this time a simple *merci beaucoup* will do.

To my mother Betty Weber Findley and my husband Carlos Leon, as well as my sisters, Sharon Dillard, Deborah Stewart, and Karrie Wroten, and my best friend Fatma Aydin Tucker, you are the people who cook for me. I've learned much from all of you. Aren't we all so lucky?

And, my work family, David, Becky, and the gang. Thanks for holding down the fort. You made it possible.

Michelle Branson you are the greatest editor in the world. I'm in awe.

Thank you Monica Pazmino for always being a source of inspiration and brilliance as you wrangled every aspect of this process to perfection. You rock.

And of course, Gibbs Smith. You made this possible and I'm forever grateful.

-Rhonda